Terrorism and 9/11
A Reader

*Edited and with an
introduction by*

Fredrik Logevall

*University of California
at Santa Barbara*

Houghton Mifflin Company   Boston   New York

Editor-in-Chief: Jean L. Woy
Sponsoring Editor: Mary Dougherty
Editorial Assistant: Noria Morales
Permissions Editor: Shirley Webster
Senior Manufacturing Coordinator: Florence Cadran
Senior Marketing Manager: Sandra McGuire

Printed in the U.S.A.

Library of Congress Control Number: 2002103098

ISBN: 0-618-25535-4

23456789-QW/F-07 06 05 04 03

Contents

Introduction

"Whether we bring our enemies to justice, or justice to our enemies, justice will be done." So declared President George W. Bush before a joint session of Congress on September 20, 2001, nine days after the most horrendous and devastating assault on the homeland in U.S. history. Three weeks later, the United States launched its war on terrorism.

Why did the attacks of 9/11 happen, and what are the implications for the world in which we live? These are the questions at the heart of this reader. The selections that follow were chosen with the intent of giving students and instructors a better grasp of the roots of the present conflict, and a surer sense of the obstacles that stand in the way of a genuine and lasting resolution of it. The authors are noted experts in their respective fields; many have devoted their careers to studying the Middle East and Central Asia. Some of the entries were written before September 11, and some after, but all add to our understanding of the key issues before us.

Immediately when the hijacked airliners crashed into the World Trade Center and the Pentagon, U.S. decision makers had to begin to fashion a response. We now know that Bush decided very early to go to war, indeed before 9/11 had become 9/12. From that first day, he also said the administration would make no distinction between the terrorists and the nations that harbored them. In the days and weeks that followed, he framed a struggle of absolutes: a campaign against evil forces, in which you were either with the United States or against it. He adopted a black-and-white approach to a campaign that, in the early months at least, garnered tremendous popular support.

But as the president surely must have known, the implications of his action were anything but simple. He had committed his administration and the nation to a complex and dangerous campaign of undefined scope and duration. The early part of the military campaign went well, as the Taliban regime in Afghanistan was swiftly routed and driven from power. As administration officials were quick to acknowledge, however, this accomplishment—though in itself of considerable importance—foretold little about what was likely to come in the months and years ahead. And on this point there has been no disagreement: the struggle against terrorism will last a long time, much longer than any one administration.

The certainty that the campaign will stretch far into the future is one reason many commentators believe it will bear a close resemblance to the Cold War, the superpower confrontation between the United States and the Soviet Union that dominated world affairs for four-plus decades after 1945. As in that earlier struggle, these observers say, the enemy is an abstraction—terrorism in place of communism—but one supported by sovereign states. Once again, the struggle will need to be fought on an ideological as well as military level, and much of it will have to be carried out through patient statecraft, espionage, and "shadow conflicts." And like in the early years of the Soviet-American confrontation, Americans today feel a sense of being threatened from within as well as externally, which almost certainly means that the war on terror will influence virtually all aspects of American life for many years to come. It will shape our spending priorities, our college curricula, our popular culture.

Other observers question the utility of the Cold War analogy. For them, there are two important differences between the two conflicts that ultimately trump any similarities. First, whereas the Cold War had a definable end—the collapse of the Soviet Union, or at least its transformation into something that no longer posed a security threat to the United States and the West—the war on terrorism does not, indeed cannot. It is a goal without a goal line—or, to change the metaphor, a disease that can be controlled and suppressed, but not cured. Proponents of this view wonder if Bush, by in effect promising a total cure, is promising more than he or anyone can deliver. Is he, they wonder, setting his country and himself up to turn success into the appearance of failure?

Second, these skeptics continue, notwithstanding the deep ideological differences between the United States and the Soviet Union, the two countries had a good deal in common; there was a certain symmetry to their confrontation. The Cold War unfolded as a clash of empires, and the superpowers pursued policies abroad that were in many respects strikingly parallel, whatever their differences at home. Rules of the game developed, and were followed. The conflict was on occasion violent, and always frightening, but at the same time predictable, almost ritualistic. Contrast this with the present situation, which reflects the asymmetries of a mature great power placed on the defensive by an enemy who is weak in the traditional measurements of power—that is, who does not command the resources of a state—and who therefore has little to lose.

To what degree this enemy commands the allegiance of a lot of people will be a very large question in the months and years to come. For a struggle against terrorism is fundamentally a battle for "hearts and minds"—a phrase familiar to Americans from their country's long and bloody ordeal in Vietnam. To defeat the Taliban in Afghanistan is one thing; to win the hearts and minds of Arab-Muslim world is quite another. "Without hearts and minds one cannot obtain intelligence, and without intelligence terrorists can never be defeated," the historian Michael Howard has written. "[I]t is well known that one man's terrorist is another man's freedom fighter. Terrorists can be successfully destroyed only if public opinion, both at home and abroad, supports the authorities in regarding them as criminals rather than as heroes."

This brings us to Osama bin Laden, the apparent mastermind behind the 9/11 attacks. Much about the man and his al-Qaeda organization remains obscure. The son of a Yemeni-born construction magnate in Saudi Arabia, bin Laden was one of fifty-three children, and the seventeenth son (although he was his mother's only child). He inherited a fortune, and gained renown as a supporter of the Afghan Mujahideen in their struggle against Soviet occupation. Gradually, he developed a terrorist organization and orchestrated a series of violent attacks around the world, many of them targeting Americans. His principal aims, it appears, are to undermine the conservative, relatively weak regimes of Egypt, Jordan, and Saudi Arabia, and the Gulf States, and to end what he sees as the long history of Western humiliations of the Muslim world. Bin Laden has no armies to achieve these large ends, and must therefore rely on the ancient tactic of the weak, using terrorism to bring about political chaos and, he hopes, regime collapse.

Is bin Laden winning the battle for the hearts and minds in the Islamic world? It's hard to be sure. That millions of Muslims were appalled and outraged by the 9/11 attacks cannot be doubted; equally clear is that the vast majority of Muslims unhappy about politics in the Middle East, or about U.S. foreign policy, or about the relentless march of Western materialism, would never dream of using deadly violence to bring about change. But neither can it be denied that many in the Arab-Muslim world are quietly cheering bin Laden on, either because they don't believe he is guilty as charged, or because they do, or because they don't care. As *New York Times* columnist Thomas L. Friedman put it not long ago, many are quietly chanting, "Run, Osama, Run," hoping that he eludes the mighty American war machine. In a way, bin Laden cannot lose. If he is captured and put on trial, he gets a platform for global propaganda. If he is killed, he becomes a martyr. And if he escapes he becomes a Robin Hood who lives to fight another day.

The rise of bin Laden may have signified a change in the nature of the terrorist threat, but the phenomenon has a long history. In one form or another, terrorism has existed since the beginning of human societies across all civilizations. In the first selection, Martin Walker provides a brief account of the more recent history of the phenomenon—beginning in the late 18th century, when the word was first used. Walker, who is the chief international correspondent for United Press International, makes the important point that those terrorist groups that have survived for long periods of time have done so because the attained degree of popular political legitimacy—that is, they have held their own in the battle for hearts and minds.

In the second reading, originally published in 1990 and retaining great contemporary resonance, Bernard Lewis examines the roots of the Muslim world's difficult relations with the West. An emeritus professor of Near Eastern Studies at Princeton University and the author of numerous important studies of Arab history and culture, Lewis traces the course of the conflict, and speaks of an emerging "clash of civilizations" (a term later popularized by Harvard scholar Samuel Huntington). He is careful to note that the movement nowadays referred to as fundamentalism is not the only Islamic tradition, but he maintains it is ascendant—pious religious reformers who reject innovation in favor of a return to the sacred past have in recent decades gained influence at the expense of secularists and modernizers. John L. Esposito, in the third selection, presents a somewhat more hopeful picture of Islamic world's relations with the West, and a wider picture of Islam generally. To the question of whether Islam and democracy are compatible Esposito, founding director of the Center for Muslim-Christian Understanding at the Walsh School of Foreign Service at Georgetown, gives a firm, albeit qualified, yes. He concedes that powerful voices within Islam have maintained otherwise, but also points to those Muslims convinced that an adherence to the faith can be reconciled with modern forms of elective government.

Notwithstanding the early success of the military campaign in Afghanistan, the final outcome in that battle-scarred and desperately poor country is anything but certain. As Milton Bearden reminds us in the fourth selection, Afghanistan has historically been a "graveyard of empires." A former CIA station chief in Afghanistan in the late 1980s, Bearden provides important insights into the failure of both Britain (in the nineteenth century) and the Soviet Union (in the late twentieth) to bring the country under their control, in each case with important international ramifications. Among other things, the Soviet intervention aided the rise of Osama bin Laden, a subject treated in the next essay, by Pakistani journalist Ahmed Rashid. A longtime student of Central Asia, Rashid writes that Washington officials failed to appreciate that bin Laden and other supporters of the Mujahideen had their own agendas, which would in time turn their hatred of the USSR on their own governments and the United States.

How do we know what bin Laden believes and is trying to achieve? Partly through his writings and other pronouncements, and the testimony of those close to him, but also through the interviews he has periodically given over the years. One such interview, with ABC News correspondent John Miller, took place in late May 1998 at bin Laden's remote mountaintop camp in southern Afghanistan. Arriving in the designated hut with seven bodyguards and several close associates, and to the sound of hundreds of rounds being fired into the air, bin Laden took questions for one hour. The transcript of the interview is our sixth reading.

At the time of the Miller interview, bin Laden had been in Afghanistan for well over a year, given asylum there by the ruling Taliban regime. The Taliban had emerged as the strongest faction of the Mujahideen, and had seized control of Kabul in 1996. The leaders proclaimed their desire to set up the world's most pure Islamic state, and swiftly moved to ban frivolities such as television, music, and cinema. As part of their attempt to end all criminal activity in the country they initiated public executions and amputations. These actions would have been enough to attract international criticism, but what really generated widespread condemnation was the regime's treatment of women. A flurry of regulations was enacted forbidding girls from going to school and women from working or getting full access to health care. Journalist Jan Goodwin personally witnessed the mistreatment of Afghan women by the Taliban; in the seventh selection, she describes what she saw.

The eighth reading returns us to the broader forces shaping the current conflict. In "Jihad v. McWorld," an article originally published in 1992, that later became the basis for a book of the same title, Benjamin R. Barber examines what he refers to as the two axial principles of our time—tribalism and globalism—and finds that they have only one thing in common: "neither offers much hope to citizens looking for practical ways to govern themselves democratically."

Why were U.S. intelligence agencies caught so unaware on 9/11? After all, the Central Intelligence Agency had worked for many years to infiltrate Osama bin Laden's terrorist organization and kept close tabs on his movements. The question will be analyzed and debated for a long time, but the ninth reading (written mere weeks before the 9/11 attacks) provides important insight into the matter. In "The Counterterrorist Myth," Reuel Marc Gerecht, a former high-level CIA operative, argues that the Agency's efforts against bin Laden have been largely ineffectual and misguided. It is exceedingly difficult, Gerecht maintains, to obtain good intelligence about any tightly organized fringe groups that may be targeting the United States. As Gerecht notes, the CIA's efforts vis-à-vis bin Laden were made difficult by the complicated role played by Pakistan, whose government provided important support and training to the Taliban—and thus indirectly to bin Laden himself. Political scientist John Echevarri-Gent, a specialist on South and Central Asian politics, writes in the next selection that the Islamabad government of Pervez Musharraf has faced a very precarious domestic political scene in recent months. On the one hand, Musharraf has sought to maintain Pakistan's alignment with the United States, deemed essential for the country's economic well being as well as its strategic posture in its long-standing territorial dispute with neighboring India; on the other hand, the president is faced with a strong challenge from religious fundamentalists within Pakistan, who frown on close relations with Washington and provide a steady stream of recruits for bin Laden's organization.

One implication of Echevarri-Gent's analysis is that, regardless of what happens to bin Laden and his al-Qaeda, Pakistan's government will continue to face internal pressure from religious fundamentalists. In the same way, argues Ahmed Rashid in the next reading, militant Islamicists in Central Asia will continue to agitate and stir up trouble regardless of what happens in the short term in the war on terrorism. Taking the story beyond Afghanistan, Rashid looks at developments in neighboring Uzbekistan, Tajikistan, Kyrgyzstan, Kazakhstan, and Turkmenistan, and worries about what he finds: sizable and growing opposition to the ruling governments, and eager and committed recruits to the cause of waging jihad throughout Central Asia.

Yvonne Yazbeck Haddad, a specialist in Islamic history who teaches at the Center for Muslim-Christian Understanding at Georgetown University, concludes the volume with a look at the experience of Muslims in the West. The excerpted essay shows how Muslims have come to form sizable minority populations in the countries of Western Europe and North America, particularly over the past few decades. Haddad concludes by wondering whether the pluralism and democratic principles espoused in these countries will make room for Muslim culture "and allow its members to operate with respect and dignity," and in turn, whether the Muslim inhabitants will fully embrace those principles. If this was a large question in the late 1990s, when Haddad posed it, it looms even larger now.

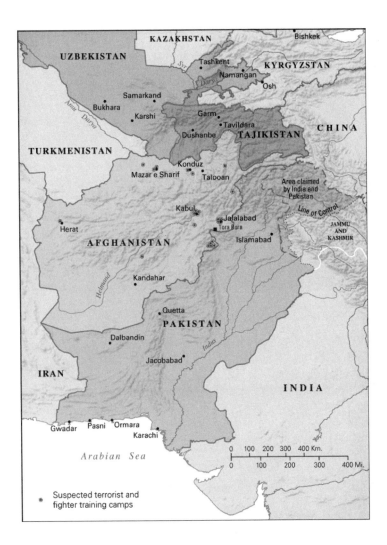

Suspected terrorist and
fighter training camps

A Brief History Of Terrorism

By Martin Walker

The word terrorism was first used in 1795, a grim spawn of the heady period that brought the American War of Independence and the French Revolution. The word was born with the Reign of Terror, the use of the guillotine by the French revolutionaries to consolidate their regime by killing their enemies and intimidating the potential opposition.

Until well into the twentieth century, terror usually meant state terror. The tactics of the French revolutionaries were copied by the Cheka secret police founded by Vladimir Lenin in 1918 to ensure the Bolshevik grip on power and later by Nazi Germany's Gestapo in the 1930s and 40s. Incidentally, it was the Nazi occupiers of Europe during the Second World War who characterized the work of the French, Czech, Polish, and other resistance movements, supplied and fomented by Britain's Special Operations Executive, as "terrorism."

For the resistance movements, and for their British backers in SOE who had been ordered by prime minister Winston Churchill to "set Europe ablaze," they were not terrorists but freedom fighters. Their clandestine work of sabotage and ambush—destroying bridges and railroads and assassinating German officials and their local collaborators—was a wholly justifiable tactic of a war of national liberation.

That was precisely the justification used after the war by a series of anticolonial movements. Some, like the Viet Minh against French rule in Vietnam, had been supplied by British and American forces to fight the Japanese. After 1945, they used the wartime tactics of resistance to attack the returning French with the classic weapons of terrorism, raiding remote plantations to kill French overseers, random shootings and bombs in crowded cafes, all designed to destroy the morale of the French civilians.

Similar tactics were used against the British in Palestine by Israeli freedom fighters (or 'terrorists') like the future prime ministers Menachem Begin and Yitzhak Shamir. The Irgun and Stern Gang blew up civilians in hotels, assassinated British troops, and ambushed British patrols, all in the name of the national liberation of Israel.

Learning from these examples, the National Liberation Front of Algeria fought French rule with a ruthless terror campaign, using Arab women dressed as fashionable young Frenchwomen, to place bombs in cafes, dancehalls, and cinemas. The French fought back ferociously, and in the battle of Algiers, General Jacques Massu's battalion of paratroopers broke the FLN terrorist networks in the casbah, or Arab quarter, with ruthless interrogations and the widespread use of torture.

The Battle of Algiers was a military victory, but a political defeat, horrifying public opinion in France and elsewhere, toppling French governments, and eroding the French national will to maintain the struggle against the FLN. France suffered a political collapse that returned to power wartime hero Charles de Gaulle, who eventually launched negotiations that led to Algerian independence in 1962.

These were the lessons that inspired modern terrorism, a phenomenon that emerged from the twin roots of the Arab-Israeli Six Day War of 1967 and the worldwide student movements of 1968. The devastating Arab defeat and the Israeli occupation of the West Bank and Gaza Strip inspired the Palestine Liberation Organization—too weak to fight an orthodox struggle—to adopt terrorist tactics. Other pro-Palestine groups imposed their demands on a global audience by hijacking airliners and kidnapping Israeli athletes at the 1972 Olympic games in Munich.

Young militants in Europe, Japan, and the United States turned to similar tactics for different reasons. In Northern Ireland, a Protestant backlash against the campaigns of the Roman Catholic civil rights movement revived the moribund Irish Republican Army. Ham-fisted attempts by the British Army to detain militants without trial triggered a thirty-year terrorist campaign.

West Germany's Red Army Faction, Japan's Red Army, and Italy's Red Brigades made common cause with the PLO. They used their training camps and cooperated on operations like the seizure of an OPEC summit meeting in Vienna in 1975, while also conducting their own kidnapping and killing operations against "the fascist capitalism" of their homelands.

This was largely a European phenomenon, despite the pinprick attacks of the Weathermen, a small group that broke away from the less extreme US antiwar movement to plant bombs in the Pentagon and elsewhere. One reason why Europe suffered far more terrorist attacks than the US was its proximity to cold war sponsors of terror, like the Czechoslovaks supplying Semtex plastic explosives to the IRA or the East German secret police, the Stasi, giving logistical support, including false passports and sanctuary, to German and Italian terror groups.

Through police and intelligence work and the ending of Soviet Bloc support with the end of the cold war, most of these post-1968 terrorist groups have been defeated or marginalized. The two that survived, the PLO and the IRA, were sustained by a degree of popular legitimacy that stemmed from their origins as national liberation movements. The two campaigns waged against them illustrate the two extremes of counter-terrorist strategy.

The British, despite ruthless bombings of civilians in London and elsewhere and repeated assassination attempts on British prime ministers, strove to maintain their civil liberties and the rule of law. Police and troops who had gone too far, or killed without cause, were put on trial. Miscarriages of justice were sometimes corrected, and outrages like the Bloody Sunday shootings by British soldiers in Londonderry in 1972 became belatedly the subject of public inquiries. By these means, and by working closely with the US and Irish government in Dublin, the British have been able to develop a peace process that brought much of the IRA back into the democratic and political arena.

The Israelis, by contrast, have assassinated PLO leaders, using bombs, missiles, and helicopter gunships despite the likelihood of civilian casualties. The Israelis, it must be stressed, believe they are fighting for their very existence, which the British are not.

However, the British and Israeli strategies represent the parameters of the counter-terror policies that the US along with its European allies and most of the civilized world, must now consider. One lesson that the Europeans all absorbed in the antiterrorism campaigns of the 1970s and 1980s is that it is both possible and important to retain civil liberties and the rule of law while fighting terrorism. One key goal of terrorism is to polarize society by provoking it into the kind of repression that undermines public support for government.

"You don't protect civilization by dismantling its civilizing achievements," comments Tom Arnold, a veteran British member of Parliament who was an adviser to former prime minister Margaret Thatcher. Arnold recalls that even after the IRA almost killed Thatcher and several cabinet colleagues by bombing her Brighton hotel during a Conservative Party conference, she rejected any new repressive measures and continued seeking a political solution with Dublin through the Anglo-Irish agreement.

Americans may question the wisdom of following the British technique when there seems to be little prospect of political negotiation with the suicidal nihilists who destroyed the World Trade Center and attacked the Pentagon. However, the ruthless Israeli tactics would not fit easily into the US political tradition and its rule of law. Possibly, the United States might adapt both strategies, echoing the British to protect civil liberties at home while being as ruthless as the Israelis abroad.

The Bush administration, however, may have few options because it will not be dealing with a 'rational' terrorist, with a clearly defined and negotiable aim like a united Ireland or a Palestinian state or an independent Algeria. There is a new cleavage between the terrorists who sought to bomb their way to the peace table, or at least to a negotiated political solution, like Arafat or Begin before him, and the implacable new fanatics like the suicide bombers of New York and Washington who simply want to blow up the peace table along with everything else. Furthermore, it is not possible to negotiate with a suicide bomber who never said what his goal was before crashing a civilian airliner into a civilian target.

The Roots of Muslim Rage

By Bernard Lewis

*Why so many Muslims deeply resent the West, and why
their bitterness will not easily be mollified.*

In one of his letters Thomas Jefferson remarked that in matters of religion "the maxim of civil government" should be reversed and we should rather say, "Divided we stand, united, we fall." In this remark Jefferson was setting forth with classic terseness an idea that has come to be regarded as essentially American: the separation of Church and State. This idea was not entirely new; it had some precedents in the writings of Spinoza, Locke, and the philosophers of the European Enlightenment. It was in the United States, however, that the principle was first given the force of law and gradually, in the course of two centuries, became a reality.

If the idea that religion and politics should be separated is relatively new, dating back a mere three hundred years, the idea that they are distinct dates back almost to the beginnings of Christianity. Christians are enjoined in their Scriptures to "render...unto Caesar the things which are Caesar's and unto God the things which are God's." While opinions have differed as to the real meaning of this phrase, it has generally been interpreted as legitimizing a situation in which two institutions exist side by side, each with its own laws and chain of authority—one concerned with religion, called the Church, the other concerned with politics, called the State. And since they are two, they may be joined or separated, subordinate or independent, and conflicts may arise between them over questions of demarcation and jurisdiction. This formulation of the problems posed by the relations between religion and politics, and the possible solutions to those problems, arise from Christian, not universal, principles and experience. There are other religious traditions in which religion and politics are differently perceived, and in which, therefore, the problems and the possible solutions are radically different from those we know in the West. Most of these traditions, despite their often very high level of sophistication and achievement, remained or became local—limited to one region or one culture or one people. There is one, however, that in its worldwide distribution, its continuing vitality, its universalist aspirations, can be compared to Christianity, and that is Islam.

Islam is one of the world's great religions. Let me be explicit about what I, as a historian of Islam who is not a Muslim, mean by that. Islam has brought comfort and peace of mind to countless millions of men and women. It has given dignity and meaning to drab and impoverished lives. It has taught people of different races to live in brotherhood and people of different creeds to live side by side in reasonable tolerance. It inspired a great civilization in which others besides Muslims lived creative and useful lives and which, by its achievement, enriched the whole world. But Islam, like other religions, has also known periods when it inspired in some of its followers a mood of hatred and violence. It is our misfortune that part, though by no means all or even most, of the Muslim world is now going through such a period, and that much, though again not all, of that hatred is directed against us.

We should not exaggerate the dimensions of the problem. The Muslim world is far from unanimous in its rejection of the West, nor have the Muslim regions of the Third World been the most passionate and the most extreme in their hostility. There are still significant numbers, in some quarters perhaps a majority, of Muslims with whom we share certain basic cultural and moral, social and political, beliefs and aspirations; there is still an imposing Western presence—cultural, economic, diplomatic—in Muslim lands, some of which are Western allies. Certainly nowhere in the Muslim world, in the Middle East or elsewhere, has American policy suffered disasters or encountered problems comparable to those in Southeast Asia or Central America. There is no Cuba, no Vietnam, in the Muslim world.... But there is a Libya, an Iran, and a Lebanon, and a surge of hatred that distresses, alarms, and above all baffles Americans.

At times this hatred goes beyond hostility to specific interests or actions or policies or even countries and becomes a rejection of Western civilization as such, not only what it does but what it is, and the principles and values that it practices and professes. These are indeed seen as innately evil, and those who promote or accept them as the "enemies of God."

This phrase, which recurs so frequently in the language of the Iranian leadership, in both their judicial proceedings and their political pronouncements, must seem very strange to the modern outsider, whether religious or secular. The idea that God has enemies, and needs human help in order to identify and dispose of them, is a little difficult to assimilate. It is not, however, all that alien. The concept of the enemies of God is familiar in preclassical and classical antiquity, and in both the Old and New Testaments, as well as in the Koran. A particularly relevant version of the idea occurs in the dualist religions of ancient Iran, whose cosmogony assumed not one but two supreme powers. The Zoroastrian devil, unlike the Christian or Muslim or Jewish devil, is not one of God's creatures performing some of God's more mysterious tasks but an independent power, a supreme force of evil engaged in a cosmic struggle against God. This belief influenced a number of Christian, Muslim, and Jewish sects, through Manichaeism and other routes. The almost forgotten religion of the Manichees has given its name to the perception of problems as a stark and simple conflict between matching forces of pure good and pure evil.

The Koran is of course strictly monotheistic, and recognizes one God, one universal power only. There is a struggle in human hearts between good and evil, between God's commandments and the tempter, but this is seen as a struggle ordained by God, with its outcome preordained by God, serving as a test of mankind, and not, as in some of the old dualist religions, a struggle in which mankind has a crucial part to play in bringing about the victory of good over evil. Despite this monotheism, Islam, like Judaism and Christianity, was at various stages influenced, especially in Iran, by the dualist idea of a cosmic clash of good and evil, light and darkness, order and chaos, truth and falsehood, God and the Adversary, variously known as devil, Iblis, Satan, and by other names.

The Rise of the House of Unbelief

In Islam the struggle of good and evil very soon acquired political and even military dimensions. Muhammad, it will be recalled, was not only a prophet and a teacher, like the founders of other religions; he was also the head of a polity and of a community, a ruler and a soldier. Hence his struggle involved a state and its armed forces. If the fighters in the war for Islam, the holy war "in the path of God," are fighting for God, it follows that their opponents are fighting against God. And since God is in principle the sovereign, the supreme head of the Islamic state—and the Prophet and, after the Prophet, the caliphs are his vicegerents—then God as sovereign commands the army. The army is God's army and the enemy is God's enemy. The duty of God's soldiers is to dispatch God's enemies as quickly as possible to the place where God will chastise them—that is to say, the afterlife.

Clearly related to this is the basic division of mankind as perceived in Islam. Most, probably all, human societies have a way of distinguishing between themselves and others: insider and outsider, in-group and out-group, kinsman or neighbor and foreigner. These definitions not only define the outsider but also, and perhaps more particularly, help to define and illustrate our perception of ourselves.

In the classical Islamic view, to which many Muslims are beginning to return, the world and all mankind are divided into two: the House of Islam, where the Muslim law and faith prevail, and the rest, known as the House of Unbelief or the House of War, which it is the duty of Muslims ultimately to bring to Islam. But the greater part of the world is still outside Islam, and even inside the Islamic lands, according to the view of the Muslim radicals, the faith of Islam has been undermined and the law of Islam has been abrogated. The obligation of holy war therefore begins at home and continues abroad, against the same infidel enemy.

Like every other civilization known to human history, the Muslim world in its heyday saw itself as the center of truth and enlightenment, surrounded by infidel barbarians whom it would in due course enlighten and civilize. But between the different groups of barbarians there was a crucial difference. The barbarians to the east and the south were polytheists and idolaters, offering no serious threat and no competition at all to Islam. In the north and west, in contrast, Muslims from an early date recognized a genuine rival—a competing world religion, a distinctive civilization inspired by that religion, and an empire that, though much smaller than theirs, was no less ambitious in its claims and aspirations. This was the entity known to itself and others as Christendom, a term that was long almost identical with Europe.

The struggle between these rival systems has now lasted for some fourteen centuries. It began with the advent of Islam, in the seventh century, and has continued virtually to the present day. It has consisted of a long series of attacks and counterattacks, jihads and crusades, conquests and reconquests. For the first thousand years Islam was advancing, Christendom in retreat and under threat. The new faith conquered the old Christian lands of the Levant and North Africa, and invaded Europe, ruling for a while in Sicily, Spain, Portugal, and even parts of France. The attempt by the Crusaders to recover the lost lands of Christendom in the east was held and thrown back, and even the Muslims' loss of southwestern Europe to the Reconquista was amply compensated by the Islamic advance into southeastern Europe, which twice reached as far as Vienna. For the past three hundred years, since the failure of the second Turkish siege of Vienna in 1683 and the rise of the European colonial empires in Asia and Africa, Islam has been on the defensive, and the Christian and post-Christian civilization of Europe and her daughters has brought the whole world, including Islam, within its orbit.

For a long time now there has been a rising tide of rebellion against this Western paramountcy, and a desire to reassert Muslim values and restore Muslim greatness. The Muslim has suffered successive stages of defeat. The first was his loss of domination in the world, to the advancing power of Russia and the West. The second was the undermining of his authority in his own country, through an invasion of foreign ideas and laws and ways of life and sometimes even foreign rulers or settlers, and the enfranchisement of native non-Muslim elements. The third—the last straw—was the challenge to his mastery in his own house, from emancipated women and rebellious children. It was too much to endure, and the outbreak of rage against these alien, infidel, and incomprehensible forces that had subverted his dominance, disrupted his society, and finally violated the sanctuary of his home was inevitable. It was also natural that this rage should be directed primarily against the millennial enemy and should draw its strength from ancient beliefs and loyalties.

Europe and her daughters? The phrase may seem odd to Americans, whose national myths, since the beginning of their nationhood and even earlier, have usually defined their very identity in opposition to Europe, as something new and radically different from the old European ways. This is not, however, the way that others have seen it; not often in Europe, and hardly ever elsewhere.

Though people of other races and cultures participated, for the most part involuntarily, in the discovery and creation of the Americas, this was, and in the eyes of the rest of the world long remained, a European enterprise, in which Europeans predominated and dominated and to which Europeans gave their languages, their religions, and much of their way of life.

For a very long time voluntary immigration to America was almost exclusively European. There were indeed some who came from the Muslim lands in the Middle East and North Africa, but few were Muslims; most were members of the Christian and to a lesser extent the Jewish minorities in those countries. Their departure for America, and their subsequent presence in America, must have strengthened rather than lessened the European image of America in Muslim eyes.

In the lands of Islam remarkably little was known about America. At first the voyages of discovery aroused some interest; the only surviving copy of Columbus's own map of America is a Turkish translation and adaptation, still preserved in the Topkapi Palace Museum, in Istanbul. A sixteenth-century Turkish geographer's account of the discovery of the New World, titled The History of Western India, was one of the first books printed in Turkey. But thereafter interest seems to have waned, and not much is said about America in Turkish, Arabic, or other Muslim languages until a relatively late date. A Moroccan ambassador who was in Spain at the time wrote what must surely be the first Arabic account of the American Revolution. The Sultan of Morocco signed a treaty of peace and friendship with the United States in 1787, and thereafter the new republic had a number of dealings, some friendly, some hostile, most commercial, with other Muslim states. These seem to have had little impact on either side. The American Revolution and the American republic to which it gave birth long remained unnoticed and unknown. Even the small but growing American presence in Muslim lands in the nineteenth century—merchants, consuls, missionaries, and teachers— aroused little or no curiosity, and is almost unmentioned in the Muslim literature and newspapers of the time.

The Second World War, the oil industry, and postwar developments brought many Americans to the Islamic lands; increasing numbers of Muslims also came to America, first as students, then as teachers or businessmen or other visitors, and eventually as immigrants. Cinema and later television brought the American way of life, or at any rate a certain version of it, before countless millions to whom the very name of America had previously been meaningless or unknown. A wide range of American products, particularly in the immediate postwar years, when European competition was virtually eliminated and Japanese competition had not yet arisen, reached into the remotest markets of the Muslim world, winning new customers and, perhaps more important, creating new tastes and ambitions. For some, America represented freedom and justice and opportunity. For many more, it represented wealth and power and success, at a time when these qualities were not regarded as sins or crimes.

And then came the great change, when the leaders of a widespread and widening religious revival sought out and identified their enemies as the enemies of God, and gave them "a local habitation and a name" in the Western Hemisphere. Suddenly, or so it seemed, America had become the archenemy, the incarnation of evil, the diabolic opponent of all that is good, and specifically, for Muslims, of Islam. Why?

Some Familiar Accusations

Among the components in the mood of anti-Westernism, and more especially of anti-Americanism, were certain intellectual influences coming from Europe. One of these was from Germany, where a negative view of America formed part of a school of thought by no means limited to the Nazis but including writers as diverse as Rainer Maria Rilke, Ernst Junger, and Martin Heidegger. In this perception, America was the ultimate example of civilization without culture: rich and comfortable, materially advanced but soulless and artificial; assembled or at best constructed, not grown; mechanical, not organic; technologically complex but lacking the spirituality and vitality of the rooted, human, national cultures of the Germans and other "authentic" peoples. German philosophy, and particularly the philosophy of education, enjoyed a considerable vogue among Arab and some other Muslim intellectuals in the thirties and early forties, and this philosophic anti-Americanism was part of the message.

After the collapse of the Third Reich and the temporary ending of German influence, another philosophy, even more anti-American, took its place—the Soviet version of Marxism, with a denunciation of Western capitalism and of America as its most advanced and dangerous embodiment. And when Soviet influence began to fade, there was yet another to take its place, or at least to supplement its working—the new mystique of Third Worldism, emanating from Western Europe, particularly France, and later also from the United States, and drawing at times on both these earlier philosophies. This mystique was helped by the universal human tendency to invent a golden age in the past, and the specifically European propensity to locate it elsewhere. A new variant of the old golden-age myth placed it in the Third World, where the innocence of the non-Western Adam and Eve was ruined by the Western serpent. This view took as axiomatic the goodness and purity of the East and the wickedness of the West, expanding in an exponential curve of evil from Western Europe to the United States. These ideas, too, fell on fertile ground, and won widespread support.

But though these imported philosophies helped to provide intellectual expression for anti-Westernism and anti-Americanism, they did not cause it, and certainly they do not explain the widespread anti-Westernism that made so many in the Middle East and elsewhere in the Islamic world receptive to such ideas.

It must surely be clear that what won support for such totally diverse doctrines was not Nazi race theory, which can have had little appeal for Arabs, or Soviet atheistic communism, which can have had little appeal for Muslims, but rather their common anti-Westernism. Nazism and communism were the main forces opposed to the West, both as a way of life and as a power in the world, and as such they could count on at least the sympathy if not the support of those who saw in the West their principal enemy.

But why the hostility in the first place? If we turn from the general to the specific, there is no lack of individual policies and actions, pursued and taken by individual Western governments, that have aroused the passionate anger of Middle Eastern and other Islamic peoples. Yet all too often, when these policies are abandoned and the problems resolved, there is only a local and temporary alleviation. The French have left Algeria, the British have left Egypt, the Western oil companies have left their oil wells, the westernizing Shah has left Iran—yet the generalized resentment of the fundamentalists and other extremists against the West and its friends remains and grows and is not appeased.

The cause most frequently adduced for anti-American feeling among Muslims today is American support for Israel. This support is certainly a factor of importance, increasing with nearness and involvement. But here again there are some oddities, difficult to explain in terms of a single, simple cause. In the early days of the foundation of Israel, while the United States maintained a certain distance, the Soviet Union granted immediate de jure recognition and support, and arms sent from a Soviet satellite, Czechoslovakia, saved the infant state of Israel from defeat and death in its first weeks of life. Yet there seems to have been no great ill will toward the Soviets for these policies, and no corresponding good will toward the United States. In 1956 it was the United States that intervened, forcefully and decisively, to secure the withdrawal of Israeli, British, and French forces from Egypt—yet in the late fifties and sixties it was to the Soviets, not America, that the rulers of Egypt, Syria, Iraq, and other states turned for arms; it was with the Soviet bloc that they formed bonds of solidarity at the United Nations and in the world generally. More recently, the rulers of the Islamic Republic of Iran have offered the most principled and uncompromising denunciation of Israel and Zionism. Yet even these leaders, before as well as after the death of Ayatollah Ruhollah Khomeini, when they decided for reasons of their own to enter into a dialogue of sorts, found it easier to talk to Jerusalem than to Washington. At the same time, Western hostages in Lebanon, many of them devoted to Arab causes and some of them converts to Islam, are seen and treated by their captors as limbs of the Great Satan.

Another explanation, more often heard from Muslim dissidents, attributes anti-American feeling to American support for hated regimes, seen as reactionary by radicals, as impious by conservatives, as corrupt and tyrannical by both. This accusation has some plausibility, and could help to explain why an essentially inner-directed, often anti-nationalist movement should turn against a foreign power. But it does not suffice, especially since support for such regimes has been limited both in extent and—as the Shah discovered—in effectiveness.

Clearly, something deeper is involved than these specific grievances, numerous and important as they may be—something deeper that turns every disagreement into a problem and makes every problem insoluble.

This revulsion against America, more generally against the West, is by no means limited to the Muslim world; nor have Muslims, with the exception of the Iranian mullahs and their disciples elsewhere, experienced and exhibited the more virulent forms of this feeling. The mood of disillusionment and hostility has affected many other parts of the world, and has even reached some elements in the United States. It is from these last, speaking for themselves and claiming to speak for the oppressed peoples of the Third World, that the most widely publicized explanations—and justifications—of this rejection of Western civilization and its values have of late been heard.

The accusations are familiar. We of the West are accused of sexism, racism, and imperialism, institutionalized in patriarchy and slavery, tyranny and exploitation. To these charges, and to others as heinous, we have no option but to plead guilty—not as Americans, nor yet as Westerners, but simply as human beings, as members of the human race. In none of these sins are we the only sinners, and in some of them we are very far from being the worst. The treatment of women in the Western world, and more generally in Christendom, has always been unequal and often oppressive, but even at its worst it was rather better than the rule of polygamy and concubinage that has otherwise been the almost universal lot of womankind on this planet.

Is racism, then, the main grievance? Certainly the word figures prominently in publicity addressed to Western, Eastern European, and some Third World audiences. It figures less prominently in what is written and published for home consumption, and has become a generalized and meaningless term of abuse—rather like "fascism," which is nowadays imputed to opponents even by spokesmen for one-party, nationalist dictatorships of various complexions and shirt colors.

Slavery is today universally denounced as an offense against humanity, but within living memory it has been practiced and even defended as a necessary institution, established and regulated by divine law. The peculiarity of the peculiar institution, as Americans once called it, lay not in its existence but in its abolition. Westerners were the first to break the consensus of acceptance and to outlaw slavery, first at home, then in the other territories they controlled, and finally wherever in the world they were able to exercise power or influence—in a word, by means of imperialism.

Is imperialism, then, the grievance? Some Western powers, and in a sense Western civilization as a whole, have certainly been guilty of imperialism, but are we really to believe that in the expansion of Western Europe there was a quality of moral delinquency lacking in such earlier, relatively innocent expansions as those of the Arabs or the Mongols or the Ottomans, or in more recent expansions such as that which brought the rulers of Muscovy to the Baltic, the Black Sea, the Caspian, the Hindu Kush, and the Pacific Ocean? In having practiced sexism, racism, and imperialism, the West was merely following the common practice of mankind through the millennia of recorded history. Where it is distinct from all other civilizations is in having recognized, named, and tried, not entirely without success, to remedy these historic diseases. And that is surely a matter for congratulation, not condemnation. We do not hold Western medical science in general, or Dr. Parkinson and Dr. Alzheimer in particular, responsible for the diseases they diagnosed and to which they gave their names.

Of all these offenses the one that is most widely, frequently, and vehemently denounced is undoubtedly imperialism.... But the way this term is used in the literature of Islamic fundamentalists often suggests that it may not carry quite the same meaning for them as for its Western critics. In many of these writings the term "imperialist" is given a distinctly religious significance, being used in association, and sometimes interchangeably, with "missionary," and denoting a form of attack that includes the Crusades as well as the modern colonial empires. One also sometimes gets the impression that the offense of imperialism is not—as for Western critics—the domination by one people over another but rather the allocation of roles in this relationship. What is truly evil and unacceptable is the domination of infidels over true believers. For true believers to rule misbelievers is proper and natural, since this provides for the maintenance of the holy law, and gives the misbelievers both the opportunity and the incentive to embrace the true faith. But for misbelievers to rule over true believers is blasphemous and unnatural, since it leads to the corruption of religion and morality in society, and to the flouting or even the abrogation of God's law....

A Clash of Civilizations

The origins of secularism in the west may be found in two circumstances—in early Christian teachings and, still more, experience, which created two institutions, Church and State; and in later Christian conflicts, which drove the two apart. Muslims, too, had their religious disagreements, but there was nothing remotely approaching the ferocity of the Christian struggles between Protestants and Catholics, which devastated Christian Europe in the sixteenth and seventeenth centuries and finally drove Christians in desperation to evolve a doctrine of the separation of religion from the state. Only by depriving religious institutions of coercive power, it seemed, could Christendom restrain the murderous intolerance and persecution that Christians had visited on followers of other religions and, most of all, on those who professed other forms of their own.

Muslims experienced no such need and evolved no such doctrine. There was no need for secularism in Islam, and even its pluralism was very different from that of the pagan Roman Empire, so vividly described by Edward Gibbon when he remarked that "the various modes of worship, which prevailed in the Roman world, were all considered by the people, as equally true; by the philosopher, as equally false; and by the magistrate, as equally useful." Islam was never prepared, either in theory or in practice, to accord full equality to those who held other beliefs and practiced other forms of worship. It did, however, accord to the holders of partial truth a degree of practical as well as theoretical tolerance rarely paralleled in the Christian world until the West adopted a measure of secularism in the late-seventeenth and eighteenth centuries.

At first the Muslim response to Western civilization was one of admiration and emulation—an immense respect for the achievements of the West, and a desire to imitate and adopt them. This desire arose from a keen and growing awareness of the weakness, poverty, and backwardness of the Islamic world as compared with the advancing West. The disparity first became apparent on the battlefield but soon spread to other areas of human activity. Muslim writers observed and described the wealth and power of the West, its science and technology, its manufactures, and its forms of government. For a time the secret of Western success was seen to lie in two achievements: economic advancement and especially industry; political institutions and especially freedom. Several generations of reformers and modernizers tried to adapt these and introduce them to their own countries, in the hope that they would thereby be able to achieve equality with the West and perhaps restore their lost superiority.

In our own time this mood of admiration and emulation has, among many Muslims, given way to one of hostility and rejection. In part this mood is surely due to a feeling of humiliation—a growing awareness, among the heirs of an old, proud, and long dominant civilization, of having been overtaken, overborne, and overwhelmed by those whom they regarded as their inferiors. In part this mood is due to events in the Western world itself. One factor of major importance was certainly the impact of two great suicidal wars, in which Western civilization tore itself apart, bringing untold destruction to its own and other peoples, and in which the belligerents conducted an immense propaganda effort, in the Islamic world and elsewhere, to discredit and undermine each other. The message they brought found many listeners, who were all the more ready to respond in that their own experience of Western ways was not happy. The introduction of Western commercial, financial, and industrial methods did indeed bring great wealth, but it accrued to transplanted Westerners and members of Westernized minorities, and to only a few among the mainstream Muslim population. In time these few became more numerous, but they remained isolated from the masses, differing from them even in their dress and style of life. Inevitably they were seen as agents of and collaborators with what was once again regarded as a hostile world. Even the political institutions that had come from the West were discredited, being judged not by their Western originals but by their local imitations, installed by enthusiastic Muslim reformers. These, operating in a situation beyond their control, using imported and inappropriate methods that they did not fully understand, were unable to cope with the rapidly developing crises and were one by one overthrown. For vast numbers of Middle Easterners, Western-style economic methods brought poverty, Western-style political institutions brought tyranny, even Western-style warfare brought defeat. It is hardly surprising that so many were willing to listen to voices telling them that the old Islamic ways were best and that their only salvation was to throw aside the pagan innovations of the reformers and return to the True Path that God had prescribed for his people.

Ultimately, the struggle of the fundamentalists is against two enemies, secularism and modernism. The war against secularism is conscious and explicit, and there is by now a whole literature denouncing secularism as an evil neo-pagan force in the modern world and attributing it variously to the Jews, the West, and the United States. The war against modernity is for the most part neither conscious nor explicit, and is directed against the whole process of change that has taken place in the Islamic world in the past century or more and has transformed the political, economic, social, and even cultural structures of Muslim countries. Islamic fundamentalism has given an aim and a form to the otherwise aimless and formless resentment and anger of the Muslim masses at the forces that have devalued their traditional values and loyalties and, in the final analysis, robbed them of their beliefs, their aspirations, their dignity, and to an increasing extent even their livelihood.

There is something in the religious culture of Islam which inspired, in even the humblest peasant or peddler, a dignity and a courtesy toward others never exceeded and rarely equalled in other civilizations. And yet, in moments of upheaval and disruption, when the deeper passions are stirred, this dignity and courtesy toward others can give way to an explosive mixture of rage and hatred which impels even the government of an ancient and civilized country—even the spokesman of a great spiritual and ethical religion—to espouse kidnapping and assassination, and try to find, in the life of their Prophet, approval and indeed precedent for such actions.

The instinct of the masses is not false in locating the ultimate source of these cataclysmic changes in the West and in attributing the disruption of their old way of life to the impact of Western domination, Western influence, or Western precept and example. And since the United States is the legitimate heir of European civilization and the recognized and unchallenged leader of the West, the United States has inherited the resulting grievances and become the focus for the pent-up hate and anger. Two examples may suffice. In November of 1979 an angry mob attacked and burned the U.S. Embassy in Islamabad, Pakistan. The stated cause of the crowd's anger was the seizure of the Great Mosque in Mecca by a group of Muslim dissidents—an event in which there was no American involvement whatsoever. Almost ten years later, in February of 1989, again in Islamabad, the USIS center was attacked by angry crowds, this time to protest the publication of Salman Rushdie's Satanic Verses. Rushdie is a British citizen of Indian birth, and his book had been published five months previously in England. But what provoked the mob's anger, and also the Ayatollah Khomeini's subsequent pronouncement of a death sentence on the author, was the publication of the book in the United States.

It should by now be clear that we are facing a mood and a movement far transcending the level of issues and policies and the governments that pursue them. This is no less than a clash of civilizations—the perhaps irrational but surely historic reaction of an ancient rival against our Judeo-Christian heritage, our secular present, and the worldwide expansion of both. It is crucially important that we on our side should not be provoked into an equally historic but also equally irrational reaction against that rival.

Not all the ideas imported from the West by Western intruders or native Westernizers have been rejected. Some have been accepted by even the most radical Islamic fundamentalists, usually without acknowledgment of source, and suffering a sea change into something rarely rich but often strange. One such was political freedom, with the associated notions and practices of representation, election, and constitutional government. Even the Islamic Republic of Iran has a written constitution and an elected assembly, as well as a kind of episcopate, for none of which is there any prescription in Islamic teaching or any precedent in the Islamic past. All these institutions are clearly adapted from Western models. Muslim states have also retained many of the cultural and social customs of the West and the symbols that express them, such as the form and style of male (and to a much lesser extent female) clothing, notably in the military. The use of Western-invented guns and tanks and planes is a military necessity, but the continued use of fitted tunics and peaked caps is a cultural choice. From constitutions to Coca-Cola, from tanks and television to T-shirts, the symbols and artifacts, and through them the ideas, of the West have retained—even strengthened—their appeal.

The movement nowadays called fundamentalism is not the only Islamic tradition. There are others, more tolerant, more open, that helped to inspire the great achievements of Islamic civilization in the past, and we may hope that these other traditions will in time prevail. But before this issue is decided there will be a hard struggle, in which we of the West can do little or nothing. Even the attempt might do harm, for these are issues that Muslims must decide among themselves. And in the meantime we must take great care on all sides to avoid the danger of a new era of religious wars, arising from the exacerbation of differences and the revival of ancient prejudices.

To this end we must strive to achieve a better appreciation of other religious and political cultures, through the study of their history, their literature, and their achievements. At the same time, we may hope that they will try to achieve a better understanding of ours, and especially that they will understand and respect, even if they do not choose to adopt for themselves, our Western perception of the proper relationship between religion and politics. To describe this perception I shall end as I began, with a quotation from an American President, this time not the justly celebrated Thomas Jefferson but the somewhat unjustly neglected John Tyler, who, in a letter dated July 10, 1843, gave eloquent and indeed prophetic expression to the principle of religious freedom:

The United States have adventured upon a great and noble experiment, which is believed to have been hazarded in the absence of all previous precedent—that of total separation of Church and State. No religious establishment by law exists among us. The conscience is left free from all restraint and each is permitted to worship his Maker after his own judgement. The offices of the Government are open alike to all. No tithes are levied to support an established Hierarchy, nor is the fallible judgement of man set up as the sure and infallible creed of faith. The Mahommedan, if he will to come among us would have the privilege guaranteed to him by the constitution to worship according to the Koran; and the East Indian might erect a shrine to Brahma if it so pleased him. Such is the spirit of toleration inculcated by our political Institutions.... The Hebrew persecuted and down trodden in other regions takes up his abode among us with none to make him afraid.... and the Aegis of the Government is over him to defend and protect him. Such is the great experiment which we have tried, and such are the happy fruits which have resulted from it; our system of free government would be imperfect without it.

The body may be oppressed and manacled and yet survive; but if the mind of man be fettered, its energies and faculties perish, and what remains is of the earth, earthly. Mind should be free as the light or as the air.

The Compatibility of Islam and Democracy

By John L. Esposito

Muslim discourse on political liberalization and democratization has embraced a broad spectrum of positions, from Muslim secularists who wish to separate religion from politics and Islamic reformers who have reinterpreted Islamic traditions in support of modern elective forms of government to those Muslims who reject democracy. Indeed, in contemporary Muslim politics Islam has often been used to legitimate democracy and dictatorship, republicanism and monarchy.

While some Islamic leaders in the past spoke out against Western-style democracy and a parliamentary system of government, this negative reaction was often part of the general rejection of European colonial influence, a defense of Islam against further dependence on the West rather than a wholesale rejection of democracy. For other Muslims, Islam is totally self-sufficient, with a divinely mandated system, based on divine sovereignty and sacred law (shariah), which is incompatible and irreconcilable with notions of popular sovereignty and civil law. Still other Muslims insist that Muslims should generate their own forms of political participation or democracy from within Islam; they have no need to look to Western forms of democracy.

The spectrum of those Muslims who believe that Islam and democracy are incompatible has been broad and diverse. In Iran during the Constitutional Movement of 1905–11, Shaykh Fadlallah Nuri, in debates over the constitution's formulation, argued that one key democratic idea—the equality of all citizens—is "impossible" in Islam. He maintained that unavoidable and insurmountable inequalities exist, such as those between believers and unbelievers, the rich and the poor, husbands and wives, the healthy and the sick, and the learned jurist and his followers. Neither is it possible for a legislative body to exist; Nuri believed that "Islam does not have any shortcomings that require completion."

Excerpted from "Contemporary Islam" by John L. Esposito. Copyright © 1999. Reprinted from *The Oxford History of Islam*, (John L. Esposito, ed.) Oxford University Press, pp. 675-690.

Sayyid Qutb, the great theoretician of the Muslim Brotherhood who was executed by the Egyptian regime in 1966, strongly objected to any notion of popular sovereignty as incompatible with God's sovereignty. Although Qutb stressed that the Islamic state must be based on the Quranic principle of consultation, he also believed that shariah is so complete as a legal and moral system that no further legislation is possible. In addition, he believed that for one group of people to legislate for others was contrary to the equality and absolute dignity of believers.

Mawlana Abul Ala Mawdudi, founder of the Jamaat-i-Islami, combined parts of Nuri's and Qutb's perspectives and yet subtly differed from them. Abul Ala Mawdudi held that Islam constitutes its own form of democracy, but he concentrated on the relationship between divine and popular sovereignty. Arguing that democracy as commonly understood is based solely on the sovereignty of the people, Abul Ala Mawdudi concluded that Islam is "the very antithesis of secular Western democracy." For this reason his critics charged that he was an "absolutist" or "doctrinal purist." Yet he went on to argue that if democracy is conceived as a limited form of popular sovereignty, restricted and directed by God's law, there is no incompatibility at all. He used the term *theodemocracy* to describe this alternative view.

This argument has resonance in the current world of Muslim political activism. For example, the constitution of the Islamic Republic of Iran, which might have been expected simply to reaffirm the absolute sovereignty of God, makes reference to both divine and popular sovereignty. Principle 2 of the constitution acknowledges that God has "the faculty to rule and implement the divine law" and that there is a "necessity to obey His orders." Yet Principle 1 indicates the hold that the idea of popular sovereignty has on modern Iranian Muslim consciousness. It notes that the Republic's government was "endorsed by the Iranian nation by an affirmative vote of 98.2 percent of the majority of eligible voters." This recognition of the central importance of political participation is further delineated in other articles in the constitution that affirm that the people should participate "in determining their political, economic, and social destiny" (Principle 3). Furthermore, the Republic should provide for a popularly elected national consultative assembly (Principle 62) and for periodic referenda on issues that are submitted "directly to the people for a judgment" (Principle 59).

More conservative voices in the Muslim world could also be heard in the 1980s and 1990s, however. In 1982 Shaykh Muhammad Mutawwali al-Sharawi, a prominent Egyptian religious leader and popular preacher whose writings and television broadcasts enjoyed an audience throughout the Arab world, created controversy by saying that Islam and democracy are incompatible and that *shura* (consultation) does not mean simple domination of the majority. In Algeria in the early 1990s the popular preacher Ali Belhadj, on of the FIS leaders, accepted participation in elections but echoed the refrain that democracy is a Judeo-Christian concept and should be replaced with inherently Islamic principles of governance. He found the concept of majority rule objectionable because issues of right and justice cannot be quantified; the greater number of votes does not translate into the greater moral position.

King Fahd of Saudi Arabia, long regarded as a conservative monarch and an ally of the West, declared that democracy is a Western institution foreign to Islam, which has its own forms of participation: "[T]he democratic system prevalent in the world is not appropriate in this region. The election system has no place in the Islamic creed, which calls for a government of advice and consultation and for the shepherd's openness to his flock, and holds the ruler fully responsible before his people."

Yet, increasingly, many Muslims have accepted the notion of democracy, although they have different opinions about its precise meaning. Muslim interpretations of democracy generally build on the well-established Quranic concept of consultation, but these interpretations vary in the degree to which "the people" are able to exercise this duty. Some argue that Islam is inherently democratic, not only because of the principle of consultation but also because of the concepts of independent reasoning (*ijtihad*) and consensus (*ijma*). The attempt to generate Islamic forms of democracy is based on a reinterpretation of traditional concepts and institutions. Consultation or political deliberation and community consensus have been reinterpreted to support parliamentary democracy, representative elections, and political parties. Thus, for example, the consultative assembly or group (*majlis al-shura*) that selected or elected a new caliph has been transformed and equated with a parliament or national assembly. As Muhammad Asad noted in *The Principles of State and Government in Islam* (1980):

> The legislative assembly—*majlis al-shura*—must be truly representative of the entire community, both men and women. Such a representative character can be achieved only through free and general elections; therefore the members of the majlis must be elected by means of the widest possible suffrage, including both men and women.

In Tunisia the group Hizb al-Nahda accepted the democratic process and sought to become a legalized political party. This commitment to pluralist politics reflected the thinking of its leader, Rashid al-Ghannoushi. He combined the criteria of Islam with that of democracy to critique the Tunisian government and to serve as a platform in Hizb al-Nahda's appeal for popular support. For al-Ghannoushi, democracy, popular sovereignty and the role of the state ("The state is not something from God but from the people...the state has to serve the benefit of the Muslims"), multiparty elections, and constitutional law are all part of a "new Islamic thinking" whose roots and legitimacy are found in a reinterpretation of Islamic sources. In affirming Hizb al-Nahda's commitment to the democratic process, al-Ghannoushi chided the West for not promoting its democratic ideals: "While the West criticizes Islamic governments for not being democratic, it also supports governments who are not democratic and are keeping Islamic movements from developing their ideas."

There are differences between Western notions of democracy and Islamic traditions. Although the great majority of Muslims today would subscribe to the idea that shura (consultative government) is central to the Islamic state, the proper relationship between popular and divine sovereignty is a subject of dispute. Most Muslims would accept that the divine will is supreme, and, in theory, that God's law is immutable and cannot be altered by human desire or whim. Yet, at the same time, by the insistence on the need of rulers to consult and to rule on the basis of consensus, Muslims effectively concede that some form of popular participation is required. Questions about the specific nature and degree of participation remain unanswered. While some Muslims debate what to call such a system, Muhammad Natsir, former Indonesian prime minister and one-time leader of the Islamically oriented Masjumi party, commented, "Islam is not one hundred percent democracy, neither is it one hundred percent autocracy. Islam is...Islam." In many places today political participation and democratization have become a litmus test by which both the openness of governments and the relevance of Islamic groups are certified. Although democracy is not entrenched in modern Islamic political thought and practice, it is a powerful symbol of legitimacy. It is used both to legitimate and to delegitimate precisely because it is seen to be a universal good.

A major hurdle facing Islamic movements today involves their willingness to tolerate diversity when in power. Some in the Muslim world and the West believe that Islamic movement participation in electoral politics is merely tactical and that once they are successful these Islamists would impose an intolerant, monolithic order on society. This issue was raised by the electoral victory of Algeria's FIS party. Despite the fact that its leader, Ali Abbasi al-Madani, affirmed his acceptance of democracy in the face of accusations that he had opposed the democratic process in the past, some of the FIS's more impatient voices—such as that of the popular preacher Ali Belhadj—unhesitatingly questioned whether democracy can be Islamic.

The record of Islamic experiments in Pakistan, Afghanistan, Iran, and Sudan raised serious issues about religious tolerance. In both Pakistan and Iran the belief that divine sovereignty naturally sets limits on the popular will has, in practice, led to a restriction on the rights of minorities and women. This is seen in the Jamaat-i-Islami's traditional hostility toward the Ahmadiyyah (a nineteenth-century messianic movement that has been criticized by the Jamaat and others and declared a non-Muslim minority in Pakistan) and advocacy of the separation of the sexes. In Pakistan, Zia-ul-Haq distinguished between democracy, which was presumably Western and objectionable, and "shurocracy" (consultative government), which was Islamic and desirable. He used Islam to legitimate martial law and banned political parties as un-Islamic. In Iran the government proved intolerant of the religious movement Bahai and its other political opponents.

In Sudan the military governments of both Jafar al-Numayri and Omar al-Bashir, in association with the Muslim Brotherhood, exacerbated the civil war by being unresponsive to criticism from the predominantly non-Muslim southerners (Animists and Christians) that imposition of the shariah discriminates against them. These examples raise serious questions about the willingness of Islamically oriented governments to tolerate dissent and to respect the rights of women and minorities. At the same time, the role of the military in Algeria, the Tunisian government's suppression of its Islamic opposition, and Egypt's crackdown on the Muslim Brotherhood to "restore democracy" by denying Islamists that which they earned or proved capable of winning in electoral politics have been equally problematic. The result in Algeria was a civil war that claimed the lives of more than seventy-five thousand people. Tunisia crushed its Islamic opposition (Hizb al-Nahda) and President Hosni Mubarak of Egypt no longer clearly distinguished between violent underground movements like the Gamaa Islamiyya and Islamic Jihad and the Muslim Brotherhood, which functioned nonviolently within society. All took control of the electoral system, banned or marginalized their Islamic opposition and indeed any significant opposition, and rigged or manipulated elections. For example, in 1993 President Ben Ali of Tunisia won reelection by 99.91 percent of the vote, and President Mubarak of Egypt took 94 percent in the 1995 elections.

Issues and Prospects for the Future

Twentieth-century Muslim history reveals a period of major religious, political, and social transformation. Amid the diversity of events and issues, fundamental questions emerge regarding religious interpretations and the authority of the past. Among them are Whose Islam? and What Islam? Both questions occur at the juncture of tradition and modernity, for contemporary Muslim societies incorporate the simultaneous presence and interplay of past, present, and future.

"Whose Islam?" Historically, rulers (caliphs and sultans) were the protectors of Islam and the ulama; by self-definition, they were the guardians and interpreters of Islam. In the second half of the twentieth century, rulers as diverse as monarchs (King Fahd of Saudi Arabia and King Hassan of Morocco), military leaders (Muammar Qaddafi, Mohammad Zia-ul-Haq, Jafar al-Numayri, and Omar al-Bashir), ex-military leaders (Anwar Sadat), and religious leaders and students (the Ayatollah Khomeini and the Taliban) have overtly used Islam to enhance their legitimacy and to mobilize popular support.

The ulama have also played a significant role in the contemporary Muslim world. The Ayatollahs Khomeini, Shariatmadari, Mutahairi, and others of Iran, Abul-Qasem Khoi of Iraq, Imam Musa Sadr and Shaykh Fadlallah of Lebanon, Muhammad al-Ghazali and Yusuf Qardawi, and many popular preachers across the Muslim world have been significant clerical voices, from masters of theology and law to social and political activists. While some wish to continue that legacy in the twentieth century, however, many if not most reformers and activists have in fact been lay rather than clerical. The Islamic modernist movement and its legacy produced generations of reformers (lay and clerical) from Egypt to Indonesia: Jamal al-Din al-Afghani, Muhammad Iqbal, Sayyid Ahmad Khan, Chiragh Ali, Allal al-Fasi, Abd al-Hamid Ben Badis, Muhammad Natsir, Prof Hamka, Muhammad Asad, many of whom often found the ulama among their sharpest critics. The major founders of neorevivalist movements, from the pioneers (Hasan al-Banna, MawlanaAbul Ala Mawdudi, Sayyid Qutb) to present-day movements, are in large part non-ulama or what some might call the new ulama or intellectuals. Laity or non-ulama are the backbone of the second and third generation of Muslim intellectuals and activists across the Muslim world, among them: Sudan's Dr. Hasan Turabi and Sadiq al-Mahdi; Tunisia's Rashid al-Ghannoushi, Iran's Ali Shariati and Abdul Karim Sorush; Algeria's Dr. Ali Abbasi al-Madani; Pakistan's Professor KhurshidAhmad; Turkey's Dr. Necmettin Erbakan; Jordan's Dr. Ishaq Farhan; Egypt's Dr. Hasan Hanafi, Kamal Aboul Magd, M. Selim al-Awa, and Fahmy Howeidy; Indonesia's Dr. Nurcholish Madjid, Abdurahman Wahid, and Dr. Deliar Noer; and Malaysia's Mohammad Kamal Hassan, Osman Bakar, and Anwar Ibrahim. They have also included women, such as Egypt's Zaynab al-Ghazali and Heba Raouf Ezzat, Pakistan's Maryam Jameelah and Riffat Hassan, Malaysia's Khalijah Mohd. Salleh, America's Amina Wadud, and others.

Both laity and the ulama write prolifically on Islamic doctrine, law, politics, science, and economics. Although there is notable cooperation among some of these activists, many continue to challenge the authority of the ulama as the sole of primary guardians of faith and belief. Emphasizing that there is no ordained clergy in Islam and that contemporary problems require a variety of experts and specialties (economics, medicine, science, and so on) that are beyond the ulama's more traditional areas of expertise, they affirm a more inclusive notion of the religious scholar or expert. As Hasan Turabi has commented: "[B]ecause all knowledge is divine and religious, a chemist, an engineer, an economist, a jurist are all ulama." Despite their common Islamic orientation, they display a diversity of intellectual positions and orientations.

The second question is *"What Islam?"* What interpretations of Islam? Islam, like all religious traditions, has been subject to multiple interpretations throughout history. Islamic tradition is the product of text and context, sacred scriptures (the Quran and Sunna of the Prophet) and sociohistorical contexts, divine revelation and human interpretation. The key issue is the relationship of tradition to modernity or postmodernity. Is the process of Islamization or re-Islamization to be based on a process of restoration or reformation, a reapplication of classical Islamic doctrine, or a reconstruction of Islamic thought that draws inspiration from the past but formulates new responses to the challenges and realities of a rapidly changing world? The issue is not change but rather how much change. How much change is necessary?

How much is permissible? What is the Islamic rationale for change? Thus, for example, although Iran was often characterized as a fundamentalist state led by a medieval, anti-Western religious figure, its government and constitution incorporated many modern concepts and institutions—including that of a republic, elected parliament, president, and prime minister—which have no clear precedent in Islamic history.

There are four discernible orientations toward change: secular, conservative (or traditionalist), neorevivalist (or fundamentalist), and neomodernist. Secularists advocate the separation of religion and politics. While their critics sometimes characterize or dismiss them as nonbelievers who represent a small westernized elite sector of society, secularists counter that they are Muslims who believe that religion should be restricted to private or personal life (prayer, fasting, personal morality). They charge that those who mix religion and politics do so for political rather than religious ends.

The three religiously oriented positions, although differing in distinct ways, nevertheless overlap because they are orientations rather than fixed, mutually exclusive positions. While each orientation may advocate a return to Islam, they differ in their presuppositions, interpretations, and methods. The conservative or traditionalist position is that of the majority of mainstream ulama, who believe that Islam is expressed quite comprehensively and adequately in classical formulations of Islamic law and doctrine. Although change can and does occur, the orientation of conservatives to past practices severely limits substantive change. Conservatives are reluctant to distinguish between revealed, immutable principles and historically conditioned laws and institutions that were the product of human reason and experience. The hold of tradition is especially reflected in those who in principle are open to reinterpretation but reflexively cling to past practices when faced with specific changes. They see no need to go back to the Quran or Sunna to develop answers to new modern problems or questions. Nor are they interested in a broad-based reformulation or reinterpretation that alters or replaces traditional Islamic laws. Thus, conservatives emphasize the following of past traditions or practices and are wary of any innovation that they regard as "deviation" (*bida*), the Muslim equivalent to Christian heresy. When change does occur, it is gradual and by way of exception in areas clearly not covered by any legal precedents. Conservatives believe that it is not the law that must change but a society that has strayed from God's path. Thus, although many ulama acquiesced to state-imposed modern, Western-inspired legal state-imposed modern, Western-inspired legal systems, it was a temporary compromise rather than an internalized change.

In the 1980s and 1990s the climate and politics of Islamic revivalism led many ulama from Egypt and Iran, to Pakistan, Bangladesh, Afghanistan, Malaysia, and Indonesia, to challenge modern reforms and call for the imposition of traditional formulations of Islamic law. However, even in these cases, beneath the ostensible unity, there has been a diversity of opinion and practice reflecting different communities (Sunni and Shii), schools of Islamic law (Hanafi, Hanbali, Jafari, Maliki, and Shafii), and local customs on such issues as women's dress and education and sexual segregation. Thus, General Zia ul-Haq's call for reimplementation of Islamic law in Pakistan set off sharp differences and conflict between Sunni and Shiite and among competing schools of Sunni religious thought. Iran's mullahs, while abrogating the shah's reformist family protection act and advocating a return to Islamic law, also bitterly criticized Afghanistan's Taliban implementation of Islamic law.

Neorevivalists or Islamists, often popularly referred to as "fundamentalists," share much in common with conservatives or traditionalists. They too emphasize a return to Islam to bring about a new renaissance. Although they respect classical formulations of Islam, they are less wedded to them. Neorevivalists claim the right to go back to Islam's original sources, to reinterpret and reapply them to contemporary society. Like conservatives, they attribute the weakness of the Islamic world primarily to the westernization of Muslim societies, the penetration of its foreign, "un-Islamic" ideas, values, and practices. In contrast to conservatives, however, they are much more flexible in their ability to adapt to change. At the same time, neorevivalists have taken issue with the Islamic modernism of Muhammad Abduh and Muhammad Iqbal, which they believe succumbed to the West and produced a westernized Islam, in their insistence that Islam is fully capable in and of itself to be the sole basis for a Muslim renaissance. Neorevivalists have produced a host of Islamic political and social movements and organizations that protest and challenge the political and religious establishments in the Muslim world, and they are often sharply critical of the West. The leadership cadre is often lay rather than clerical, graduates and professionals trained in the modern sector rather than in seminaries. They are thus more likely to be educators, journalists, scientists, physicians, lawyers, or engineers than ulama.

The earlier division of elites in many Muslim societies into modern secular or traditional (the ulama)—based on the bifurcation of education in modern, Western-oriented schools and in traditional Islamic or religious schools—is complemented today by a highly educated but more Islamically oriented sector of society, an alternative elite. The contemporary revival has also produced a new generation of Islamic reformers: neomodernists, who seek to bridge the gap between the traditionally and the secularly educated. They too are activists who look to the early Islamic period as embodying the normative ideal. Although they overlap with neorevivalists or Islamists, with whom they are often grouped, neomodernists are more flexible and creative in their thought. After an early traditional education, many obtain degrees from Western-oriented national universities or at major universities in the West. They emphasize the importance of "Islamic modernization and development." This new sector has produced a diverse group of leaders and intellectuals.

Islamic neomodernists do not reject the West in its entirety; rather, they choose to be selective in approach. They wish to appropriate the best of science, technology, medicine, and intellectual thought but to resist acculturation or the assimilation of Western culture and mores, from secularism and radical individualism to the breakdown of the family and sexual permissiveness. The goal is thus to learn from the West but not to westernize Muslim society. The distinction is drawn between the rejection of change (modernization) and the uncritical, indiscriminate, blind imitation of the West.

Contemporary Islamic reformers or neomodernists also stress the need to renew Islam both at the individual and the community levels. They advocate a process of Islamization or re-Islamization that begins with the sacred sources of Islam, the Quran and Sunna of the Prophet, but that also embraces the best in other cultures. They see themselves as engaging in a dynamic process that is as old as Islam itself. Much as early Muslims interpreted and applied Islamic principles and values to their times and adopted and adapted political, legal, and economic practices from the cultures they had conquered, the neomodernist reformers wish to bring about a new Islamic renaissance (*nahda*) pursuing a similar selective, self-critical path. They distinguish between God's revelation and human interpretations, between that part of Islamic law which is eternal and that which is contingent and relative, between immutable principles and regulations that were human constructs conditioned by time and place. In contrast to neorevivalists, neomodernists are more creative and wide-ranging in their reinterpretation of Islam and less tied to traditional interpretations of the ulama. For this reason, they are often accused of "deviationism" by the ulama, who charge that neomodernists lack the necessary training and credentials to interpret Islam.

Contemporary Muslim Societies: Old and New Realities

Islam in the twentieth century has been associated with reformation and revolution. Political and intellectual movements responded to the challenge of European colonialism, achieved independence, and established modern Muslim states and societies. In the last decades of the twentieth century, a second struggle emerged. This Islamic resurgence signals both the failures of Muslim societies and deep-seated, unresolved religio-cultural issues, as Muslims continue to struggle with the meaning and relevance of Islam in the world today. The issues have extended from textual criticism and interpretation of the Quran and Prophetic traditions to the role of religion in state and society. This resurgence has yielded a variety of questions, from the nature of the state and Islamic law to pluralism and the status and rights of women and minorities.

Although the Quran and Sunna of the Prophet Muhammad remain normative for most Muslims, questions of interpretation, authenticity, and application have become contentious items. Some Muslims see little need to substantially redefine past approaches and practices; others strike out into new territory. Some Muslim scholars distinguish the eternal, immutable principles and laws in the Quran from those prescriptions that are contingent responses to specific contexts. Other scholars distinguish between the Meccan and Medinan *suras* (chapters): the Meccan chapters are regarded as the earlier and more religiously binding texts; the Medinan are seen as primarily political, concerned with Muhammad's creation of the Medinan state and therefore not universally binding. Still other Muslim scholars have distinguished between the Quran's eternal principles and values, which are to be applied and reapplied to changing sociopolitical contexts, and past legislation that was primarily intended for specific historical periods.

Although the example of the Prophet Muhammad has always been normative in Islam, from earliest times Muslim scholars saw the need to critically examine and authenticate the enormous number of hadith (Prophetic traditions), to distinguish between authoritative texts and pious fabrications. In the twentieth century a sector of modern Western scholarship questioned the historicity and authenticity of the hadith, maintaining that the bulk of the Prophetic traditions were written much later. Most Muslim scholars and some Western (non-Muslim) scholars have taken exception with this sweeping position. Many ulama continue to unquestioningly accept the authoritative collections of the past; other Muslim scholars have in fact become more critical in their approaches and uses of hadith literature.

New approaches to the study and interpretation of Islam's sacred sources have been accompanied by similar debates over the nature of Islamic law, the shariah. As noted, many ulama continue to equate the shariah with its exposition in legal manuals developed by the early law schools. Other Muslims—from Islamic modernists such as Muhammad Abduh, Sayyid Ahmad Khan, and Muhammad Iqbal to Islamic revivalists and neomodernists—have distinguished between those laws based on clear texts of the Quran and hadith and those that are the product of human interpretation and application, the product of reason and custom. Some express this distinction as that between the eternal law of God (shariah) and its human interpretation and application (*fiqh*) by early jurists. The distinction is often articulated in terms of the classical division of law into a Muslim's duties or obligations to God (*ibadat*, worship) and his or her duties to others (*muamalat*, social obligations). The former (for example, the performance of the Five Pillars of Islam, the essential beliefs and practices) are seen as unchanging; the latter are contingent upon historical and social circumstances.

Contemporary Muslim discussion and debate over the role of Islam in state and society reflect a broad array of questions: Is there one classical model or many possible models for the relationship of religion to political, social, and economic development? If a new Islamic synthesis is to be achieved that provides continuity with past tradition, how will this be accomplished, imposed from above by rulers and the ulama or legislated from below through a representative electoral process?

Legal reform remains a contested issue in many Muslim communities. Many emerging Muslim states followed a pattern of implementing Western-inspired legal codes. The process of legal change did not reflect widespread social change so much as the desires of a small secular-oriented sector of the population. Governments imposed reforms from above through legislation. The process, contradictions, and tensions inherent in modernization programs in most Muslim societies were starkly reflected in family law (marriage, divorce, and inheritance) reforms. Family law, which is regarded as the heart of the shariah and the basis for a strong, Islamically oriented family structure and society, was the last area of law to be touched by reformers. Even then, unlike most areas of law that implemented Western-inspired legal systems and codes, Muslim family law was not displaced or replaced but instead subjected to selective reform. Officials often employed an Islamic modernist rationale, in an ad hoc and haphazard manner, to provide an Islamic facade and legitimacy.

Family law ordinances were drawn up and implemented by the state, not by the ulama, pitting religious leaders against both secular and Islamic modernists. The ulama tended to object to any tampering with Islamic law, maintaining that (1) they and they alone were the qualified experts in Islamic doctrine and law; (2) the law was sacred and unchangeable; and (3) modernists were unduly influenced by the West and thus family law reforms were simply an illegitimate attempt to "westernize" God's law. However, the government imposed reforms that were ultimately accepted, albeit reluctantly. Modernizing elites accommodated the force of tradition in their unwillingness to directly challenge or invalidate classical Islamic law. Thus, violation of the law did not render an act invalid, only illegal. Moreover, punishments in the form of fines and imprisonment for men who ignored reforms that limited their right to polygamous marriages or to divorce were often minimal. The contemporary resurgence of Islam triggered the ulama's reassertion of the authority of the past, as they called for a return to the shariah and sought to repeal family law reforms and reassert classical, medieval formulations of Muslim family law.

In more recent decades, the debate over whether the shariah should be part of or the basis of a country's legal system has become a sensitive, and at times contentious, issue. If it should be, to what degree? Does Islamization of law mean the wholesale reintroduction of classical law, the development of new laws derived from the Quran and Sunna of the Prophet, or simply the acceptance of any law that is not contrary to Islam? Who is to oversee this process: rulers, the ulama, parliaments? As Iran, Sudan, Afghanistan, Pakistan, and Saudi Arabia demonstrate, the implementation of shariah has not followed a fixed pattern or set interpretation even among those dubbed conservative or fundamentalist. For example, women in Saudi Arabia and Afghanistan under the Taliban cannot vote or hold public office. In Pakistan and Iran, despite other strictures and problems, women vote, hold political office in parliaments and cabinets, teach in universities, and hold responsible professional positions. However, Islamization of law has underscored several areas that have proved particularly problematic: the *hudud* (punishments as prescribed by the Quran and hadith for certain crimes, such as alcohol consumption, theft, fornication, adultery, and false witness) and the status of non-Muslims (*dhimmi*), minorities, and women. All involve the question of change in Islamic law.

Although many traditionalists and neorevivalists or fundamentalists call for the reimplementation of the hudud punishments, other Muslims argue that they are no longer appropriate. Among those who advocate imposition of the hudud (for example, amputation for theft or stoning for adultery), some call for its immediate introduction and others argue that such punishments are contingent upon the creation of a just society in which people are not driven to steal in order to survive. Some critics charge that although appropriate relative to the time period in which they were introduced, hudud punishments are unnecessarily harsh in a modern context. Although many Muslim rulers and governments try to avoid directly addressing the issue of the hudud, Prime Minister Mahathir Mohamad of Malaysia, advocate of a modernized Malaysia with a moderate, tolerant Islam, directly criticized the conservatism of his country's ulama, their legal opinions (*fatwas*), and religious courts. In addition, he refused to allow the Malaysian state of Kelantan, the only state controlled by PAS (the Islamic Party of Malaysia), an Islamic opposition political party, to implement the hudud.

The reintroduction of Islamic law has often had a particularly pronounced negative impact on the status and role of women and minorities, raising serious questions about whether it constitutes a setback in the gains made in many societies. During the postindependence period, significant changes occurred in many countries, broadening the educational and employment opportunities and enhancing the legal rights of Muslim women. Women became more visible in the professions (as teachers, lawyers, engineers, physicians) and in government. Admittedly, these changes affected only a small proportion of the population and varied from one country or region to another, influenced by religious and local traditions, economic and educational development, and government leadership. The contrasts could be seen from Egypt and Malaysia to Saudi Arabia and Iran.

One result of contemporary Islamic revivalism has been a reexamination of the role of women in Islam, and at times a bitter debate over their role in society. More conservative religious voices among the ulama and Islamists have advocated a return to veiling and sexual segregation as well as restricting women's education and employment. Muslim women are regarded as culture bearers, teachers

Muslim women are regarded as culture bearers, teachers of family faith and values, whose primary roles as wives and mothers limit or exclude participation in public life. The imposition of reputed Islamic laws by some governments and the policies of some Islamist movements reinforced fears of a retreat to the past: in Afghanistan, the Taliban enforcement of veiling, closure of women's schools, restriction of women in the workplace; in Pakistan, General Zia ul-Haq's reintroduction of the hudud punishments and a law that counted women's testimony as half that of men's; greater restrictions on women in the Islamic Republics of Iran and Sudan; the murderous brutality of Algeria's Armed Islamic Group toward unveiled or more westernized professional women. In fact, the picture is far more complex and diverse, revealing both old and new patterns.

Muslim women in the twentieth century had two clear choices or models before them: the modern westernized lifestyle common among an elite minority of women or the more restrictive traditional "Islamic" lifestyle of the majority of women, who lived much the same as previous generations. The social impact of the Islamic revival, however, produced a third alternative that is both modern and firmly rooted in Islamic faith, identity, and values. Muslim women, modernists, and Islamists have argued on Islamic grounds for an expanded role for women in Muslim societies. Distinguishing between Islam and patriarchy, between revelation and its interpretation by the (male) ulama in patriarchal settings, Muslim women have reasserted their right to be primary participants in redefining their identity and role in society; In many instances, this change has been symbolized by a return to the wearing of Islamic dress. This has not simply meant a wholesale return to traditional Islamic forms of dress, however. For some it is the donning of a head scarf (*hijab*); others from Cairo to Kuala Lumpur have adopted new forms of Islamic dress, modest but stylish, worn by students and professionals. Initially prominent primarily among urban middle-class women, this new mode of dress has become more common among a broader sector of society. For many it is an attempt to combine religious belief and values with contemporary levels of education and employment, to subordinate a much-desired process of social change to indigenous, Islamic values and ideals. The goal is a more authentic rather than simply westernized modernization.

Islamic dress has the practical advantage of enabling some women to assert their modesty and dignity while functioning in public life in societies in which Western dress often symbolizes a more permissive lifestyle. It creates a protected, private space of respectability in crowded urban environments. For some it is a sign of feminism that rejects what they regard as the tendency of women in many Muslim societies to go from being defined as sexual objects in a male-dominated tradition to being exploited as sexual objects Western-style. Western feminism is often seen as a liberation that has resulted in a new form of bondage to dress, youthfulness and physical beauty, sexual permissiveness and exploitation, a society in which women's bodies are used to sell every form of merchandise from clothing to automobiles and cellular phones. Covering the body, it is argued, defines a woman and gender relations in society in terms of personality and talents rather than physical appearance.

Contemporary Muslim societies reflect both the old and the new realities. Traditional patterns remain strong and are indeed reasserted and defended by those who call for a more widespread return to tradi-tional forms of Islamic dress and sexual segregation or seclusion (pur-dah) in public life. At the same time, however, Muslim women have also become catalysts for change, empowering themselves by entering the professions, running for elective office and serving in parliament (in countries as diverse as Egypt and Iran), becoming students and scholars of Islam, conducting their own women's study groups, and establishing women's professional organizations, journals, and magazines. Women's organizations from Egypt and Iran to Pakistan and Indone-sia—such as Women Living Under Muslim Laws, based in Pakistan but international in membership, and Malaysia's Sisters in Islam—are active internationally in protecting and promoting the rights of Muslim women.

The simultaneous call for greater political participation and for more Islamically oriented societies has not only had a negative impact on non-Muslim communities, but it has also sparked a lively discussion and debate among Muslim intellectuals and religious leaders over the status of non-Muslims in an Islamic state. The traditional doctrine of non-Muslims as "protected people," enabling many to practice their faith and hold positions in society, was advanced relative to its times and to the then far more exclusive approach of Western Christendom. By modern standards of pluralism and equality of citizenship, however, it amounts to second-class status. More conservative Muslim voices continue to celebrate and defend this doctrine, while other Muslims from Egypt to Indonesia have advocated a redefinition of the status of non-Muslims, in terms of their right to full and equal citizenship, which would enable an egalitarian and pluralist society of Muslims and non-Muslims. This is reflected in debates in Egypt over whether the Copts can serve in the army or should have to pay a special tax and similar discussions about issues of religious and political pluralism in countries such as Lebanon, Pakistan, Malaysia, and Indonesia.

Ironically, questions of citizenship and the exercise of political rights have become increasingly significant for Muslim minority communities in the second half of the twentieth century. At no time in history have Muslim minorities been as numerous and widespread. Both the swelling numbers of Muslim refugees and the migration of many Muslims to Europe, Canada, South America, and the United States, where Islam is now the second or third largest religion, make the issue of minority rights and duties within the majority community an ever-greater concern for Islamic jurisprudence. Can Muslim minority communities accept full citizenship and participate fully politically and socially within non-Muslim majority communities that are not governed by Islamic law? What is the relationship of Islamic law to civil law? What is the relationship of culture to religion? Are Muslims who live in the United States American Muslims or Muslims in America? How does one distinguish between culture and religion, that is, between the essentials of Islam and its cultural (Egyptian, Pakistani, Sudanese, Indonesian) expressions?

The history of Islam in the contemporary world, as throughout much of history, continues to be one of dynamic change. Muslim societies have experienced the effects of rapid change, and with it the challenges in religious, political, and economic development. Muslims continue to grapple with the relationship of the present and future to the past. Like believers in their sister traditions, Judaism and Christianity, the critical question is the relationship of faith and tradition to change in a rapidly changing and pluralistic world. As Fazlur Rahman, a distinguished Muslim scholar, observed in *Islam and Modernity* (1982), Muslims need "some first-class minds who can interpret the old in terms of the new as regards substance and turn the new into the service of the old as regards ideals."

Afghanistan, Graveyard of Empires

By Milton Bearden

The Great Game

Michni Point, Pakistan's last outpost at the western end of the barren, winding Khyber Pass, stands sentinel over Torkham Gate, the deceptively orderly border crossing into Afghanistan. Frontier Scouts in gray shalwar kameezes (traditional tunics and loose pants) and black berets patrol the lonely station commanded by a major of the legendary Khyber Rifles, the militia force that has been guarding the border with Afghanistan since the nineteenth century, first for British India and then for Pakistan. This spot, perhaps more than any other, has witnessed the traverse of the world's great armies on campaigns of conquest to and from South and Central Asia. All eventually ran into trouble in their encounters with the unruly Afghan tribals.

Alexander the Great sent his supply trains through the Khyber, then skirted northward with his army to the Konar Valley on his campaign in 327BC. There he ran into fierce resistance and, struck by an Afghan archer's arrow, barely made it to the Indus River with his life. Genghis Khan and the great Mughal emperors began passing through the Khyber a millennium later and ultimately established the greatest of empires—but only after reaching painful accommodations with the Afghans. From Michni Point, a trained eye can still see the ruins of the Mughal signal towers used to relay complex torch-light messages 1,500 miles from Calcutta to Bukhara in less than an hour.

In the nineteenth century the Khyber became the fulcrum of the Great Game, the contest between the United Kingdom and Russia for control of Central Asia and India. The first Afghan War (1839-42) began when British commanders sent a huge army of British and Indian troops into Afghanistan to secure it against Russian incursions, replacing the ruling emir with a British protégé. Facing Afghan opposition, by January 1842 the British were forced to withdraw from Kabul with a column of 16,500 soldiers and civilians, heading east to the garrison at Jalalabad, 110 miles away. Only a single survivor of that group ever made it to Jalalabad safely, though the British forces did recover some prisoners many months later.

According to the late Louis Dupree, the premier historian of Afghanistan, four factors contributed to the British disaster: the occupation of Afghan territory by foreign troops, the placing of an unpopular emir on the throne, the harsh acts of the British-supported Afghans against their local enemies, and the reduction of the subsidies paid to the tribal chiefs by British political agents. The British would repeat these mistakes in the second Afghan War (1878-81), as would the Soviets a century later; the United States would be wise to consider them today.

In the aftermath of the second British misadventure in Afghanistan, Rudyard Kipling penned his immortal lines on the role of the local women in tidying up the battlefields:

> *When you're wounded and left on Afghanistan's plains*
> *And the women come out to cut up what remains*
> *Jest roll to your rifle an' blow out your brains*
> *An' go to your Gawd like a soldier.*

The British fought yet a third war with Afghanistan in 1917, an encounter that neither burnished British martial history nor subdued the Afghan people. But by the end of World War I, that phase of the Great Game was over. During World War II, Afghanistan flirted with Aryanism and the Third Reich, becoming, fleetingly, "the Switzerland" of Central Asia in a new game of intrigue as Allied and Axis coalitions jockeyed for position in the region. But after the war the country settled back into its natural state of ethnic and factional squabbling. The Soviet Union joined in from the sidelines, but Afghanistan was so remote from the consciousness of the West that scant attention was paid to it until the last king, Zahir Shah, was deposed in 1973. Then began the cycle of conflict that continues to the present.

Russian Roulette

Afghanistan festered through the 1970s, but with the seizure of power in Kabul by Nur Mohammed Taraki in 1978, the country began a rapid spiral into anarchy. Washington's ambassador in Kabul, Adolph Dubs, was kidnapped in February 1979 and later killed during a failed rescue attempt; the next month, Hafizullah Amin seized the prime ministership along with much of Taraki's power; and eight months later, on Christmas Eve, after watching the disintegration of order for much of a decade, the Kremlin decided to try its hand at military adventure.

The Soviets began with a modern repetition of the fatal British error of installing an unpopular "emir" on the Afghan "throne." The operation was marked by a brutal efficiency: Hafizullah Amin was killed under mysterious circumstances, Kabul was secured, and the Soviets put their man, Babrak Karmal, at the helm of the Afghan government. It looked initially as if the Soviets' optimistic prediction that they would be in and out of Afghanistan almost before anyone noticed might prove correct. Certainly, President Jimmy Carter was too preoccupied with the hostage crisis in Iran to give much thought to Afghanistan, or so the Kremlin believed.

To Moscow's surprise, however, Carter reacted quickly and decisively. He cancelled a number of pending agreements with the Soviet Union, ranging from wheat sales to consular exchanges; he set in motion the boycott of the 1980 Moscow Olympics; and, much more quietly and decisively, he signed a presidential finding that tasked the CIA with the organization of aid, including arms and military support, to the Afghan people in their resistance to the Soviet occupation. In January 1980, Carter sent his national security adviser, Zbigniew Brzezinski, for consultations with Pakistani leaders who were already supporting the Afghan resistance. On a side trip from Islamabad, Brzezinski traveled the length of the Khyber Pass to the outpost at Michni Point, where he was photographed squinting along the sights of a Soviet AK-47 assault rifle, its muzzle elevated and pointing into Afghanistan. In that moment, the president's national security adviser became the symbol of the impending U.S. phase of involvement in Afghanistan's endless martial history.

The CIA had to scramble to comply with the president's order. But within weeks it had organized its first weapons delivery—a shipment of several thousand venerable Enfield .303 rifles, the standard weapon of the Afghan tribals—to the resistance fighters who were already beginning to snipe at the Soviet invaders. During the 1980s, the agency would deliver several hundred thousand tons of weapons and ordnance to Pakistan for distribution to the Afghan fighters known to the world as mujahideen, the soldiers of God. The coalition of countries supporting the resistance grew to an impressive collection that included the United States, the United Kingdom, Pakistan, Saudi Arabia, Egypt, and China. Lining up behind seven separate and fractious Afghan resistance leaders based in Peshawar, the capital of Pakistan's Northwest Frontier Province, the mujahideen field commanders were allotted their supplies and sent off to face the Soviet forces.

For the first five years of its covert war, the CIA attempted to maintain plausible deniability. Its officers in Pakistan kept a low profile, and the weapons it supplied to the mujahideen, with the exception of the British Enfields, were models manufactured in Warsaw Pact countries. An additional advantage of using Soviet bloc weapons was that the mujahideen could use any ammunition they could capture from army garrisons of the puppet Democratic Republic of Afghanistan—or buy, with American dollars, from corrupt DRA quartermasters or even Red Army supply officers.

By 1985, the Soviet 40th Army had grown from its original, limited expeditionary force to an occupation force of around 120,000 troops, widely dispersed at garrisons around the country. But as the Soviet forces grew, so did the Afghan resistance. By the mid-1980s the mujahideen had more than 250,000 full- or part-time fighters in the field, and though they and the civilian population had suffered horrendous losses—a million dead and 1.5 million injured, plus 6 million more driven into internal and external exile—the Soviet forces were also beginning to suffer.

As the CIA became more deeply involved in its covert proxy war with the Soviet Union, it became clear to President Ronald Reagan's new CIA director, William Casey, that the conflict had stalemated. The United States was fighting the Soviets to the last Afghan in a confrontation that could run on indefinitely. By 1985 Soviet air tactics had been refined, and the mujahideen suffered increasing casualties from the growing Soviet fleet of heavily armored MI-24d attack helicopters. The Afghans had nothing in their arsenal adequate to defend against this equipment and so, after a heated debate and heavy pressure from Congress, the White House decided to provide them with Stinger antiaircraft missiles. The Stingers entered the war a month after Mikhail Gorbachev's seminal August 1986 speech in Vladivostok, where he described the conflict, now in its seventh year, as a "bleeding wound." U.S. intelligence at the time, however, indicated that as he uttered those first words of disengagement, he also gave his generals one year to bring the Afghans under control, using whatever force necessary. Three months earlier the Soviets had replaced the failing Babrak Karmal with the brutal, sadistic secret-police chief Mohammed Najibullah, a move that only stiffened mujahideen resistance and set the scene for the end-game of the Soviets' Afghan adventure.

Two events in the late summer of 1986 changed the course of the war. On August 20 a lucky shot by the mujahideen sent a 107 mm rocket into a DRA supply dump on the outskirts of Kabul, setting off secondary explosions that destroyed tens of thousands of tons of ordnance, lighting up the skies of the Afghan capital by night and smoldering during the day. A month later, on September 26, a team led by a resistance commander with the unlikely name of Ghaffar ("the forgiver," one of the 99 names of Allah) brought down three MI-24 helicopters in the first Stinger ambush of the war. The effect of these events on the mujahideen was electric, and within days the setbacks for the Soviet forces were snowballing, with one or two aircraft per day falling from the skies at the end of the Stingers' telltale white plumes.

When the snows melted in the high passes for the new fighting season of 1987, diplomatic activity intensified, with the United States represented by the exceptionally able Michael Armacost, the undersecretary of state for political affairs. It had become clear not only to Gorbachev and his negotiators but also to his generals in the field that there would be no letup in Afghanistan, and that the time to consider disengagement had come. On April 14, 1988, after agonized negotiations over such tortured concepts as "negative symmetry" in drawing down supplies to the combatants, the Geneva Accords ending Soviet involvement in Afghanistan were signed. The date for the final withdrawal of all Soviet forces was set at February 15, 1989, a timetable that the commander of the Soviet 40th Army in Afghanistan, General Boris Gromov, choreographed to the last moment of the last day. February 15 also marked the end of outside military support to both sides in the war, at least in theory.

Gromov wanted arrangements to be just right. The international press was shuttled from nearby Termez, Uzbekistan, to a special press center, complete with a new, covered pavilion. The body of a hapless minesweeper had been quietly carried across the Friendship Bridge before the press had time to reason that his blanket-wrapped form was the last Russian soldier killed in the ten-year war. The cameras of several dozen news services zoomed in on the center of the bridge, where a lone Soviet tank had pulled to a halt. The diminutive Soviet general jumped from the turret, pulled his battle-dress tunic into place, and strode purposely over the last hundred yards toward the Soviet side of the Amu Dar'ya. Just before he reached the end of the bridge, his son Maksim, a slim, awkward 14-year-old, greeted his father with a stiff embrace and presented him with a bouquet of red carnations. Son and father marched the last 50 yards out of Afghanistan together.

Arabian Knights

In ten years of war, the Soviet Union admitted to having had about 15,000 troops killed in action, several hundred thousand wounded, and tens of thousands dead from disease. The true numbers might be higher, but they are not worth debating. What followed Gromov's exit grew rapidly into a cataclysm for the Soviets and a national disaster for the Afghans.

The first signs came in May 1989, when an already emboldened Hungarian government correctly concluded it could open its border with Austria without fear of Soviet intervention. That signal act was followed a month later by the stunning election of a Solidarity majority in Poland's parliament, ending that country's nearly half-century of communist rule. Throughout the summer of 1989, the people of East Germany took to the streets, first in small numbers, then gaining strength and courage in the tens and hundreds of thousands until, on the night of November 9, 1989, in a comedy of errors and miscues, the Berlin Wall was breached and Germans surged from east to west. The world had hardly digested these events when Czechoslovakia's Vaclav Havel and his band of dissidents from the Magic Lantern theater carried out their own Velvet Revolution a month later.

With the world's eyes focused almost exclusively on the historic events in Eastern Europe, or on the vivid image of a young demonstrator staring down a Chinese tank in Beijing's Tiananmen Square, the drama unfolding in Afghanistan received scant attention. Though there were heroic efforts by relief agencies to provide humanitarian aid, the senior officials of President George H. W. Bush's administration did not look back to that former war zone, their energies instead consumed by the stunning denouement of the Cold War.

In the turn away from Afghanistan, the United States would dismiss even its staunch ally, Pakistan. No longer able to stave off congressionally mandated sanctions triggered by its nuclear weapons development program, Pakistan fell out of Washington's favor. As the 1990s began with great hope elsewhere in the world, in Afghanistan a new post-Cold War construct started taking shape: the failed state. And as it failed and spun into anarchy, Afghanistan became the home of a new and little understood threat: the aggrieved Arab extremist.

The role of the so-called Afghan Arabs in the ten-year war against the Soviet occupation is the subject of much debate and misinformed commentary. By early 1980, the call to jihad (holy war) had reached all corners of the Islamic world, attracting Arabs young and old and with a variety of motivations to travel to Pakistan to take up arms and cross the border to fight against the Soviet invaders in Afghanistan. There were genuine volunteers on missions of humanitarian value, there were adventure seekers looking for paths to glory, and there were psychopaths. As the war dragged on, a number of Arab states discreetly emptied their prisons of homegrown troublemakers and sent them off to the jihad with the fervent hope that they might not return. Over the ten years of war as many as 25,000 Arabs may have passed through Pakistan and Afghanistan. At one time the CIA considered having volunteer Arab legions take part in the war, but the idea was scrapped as unwise and unworkable. Despite what has often been written, the CIA never recruited, trained, or otherwise used the Arab volunteers who arrived in Pakistan. The idea that the Afghans somehow needed fighters from outside their culture was deeply flawed and ignored basic historical and cultural facts. The Arabs who did travel to Afghanistan from Peshawar were generally considered nuisances by mujahideen commanders, some of whom viewed them as only slightly less bothersome than the Soviets. As fundraisers, however, the Arabs from the Persian Gulf played a positive, often critical role in the background of the war. During some months in 1987 and 1988, Arab fundraisers in both Pakistan and their home countries raised as much as $25 million for their largely humanitarian and construction projects. Among the more prominent of these Arab fundraisers was one Osama bin Ladin, the son of a Saudi billionaire.

Active in Afghanistan since the early 1980s, having previously worked in the Persian Gulf to recruit Arabs for the jihad, bin Ladin focused his early energies on construction projects, building orphanages and homes for widows as well as roads and bunker systems in eastern Afghanistan. He and a few of his Saudi followers saw some combat in 1987, while associated with the Islamic Unity Party of Abdul Rasul Sayaf, an Egyptian-trained Afghan member of the Muslim Brotherhood who later in the jihad embraced Saudi Wahhabism. At the crucial battles of Jaji and Ali Khel, Sayaf and his Saudis acquitted themselves well by stopping a Soviet and DRA advance that could have resulted in large-scale destruction of mujahideen supply dumps and staging areas in the province of Paktia. More than two dozen Saudis died in those engagements, and the military legend of Osama bin Ladin was born.

But at this point in the war, few were concerned about the role of the Afghan Arabs, with the exception of growing criticism by Western humanitarian organizations of the harsh fundamentalism of the Saudi Wahhabis and Deobandis whose influence in the refugee camps in Pakistan, now bursting with about three million Afghans, was pervasive. It was in these squalid camps that a generation of young Afghan males would be born into and raised in the strictest fundamentalism of the Deobandi madrassas (Islamic schools). It was here that the seeds of the Taliban were sown.

Come, Mr. Taliban

Though the Soviets left Afghanistan in 1989, it was not until April 1992 that the mujahideen finally took Kabul, killed Najibullah, and declared what passed for victory. Their triumph would be short-lived. Old hatreds and ethnic realities once again drove events, and without the unifying presence of foreign armies on Afghan soil, the state of Afghanistan simply fell apart. The civil war resumed with horrendous brutality until the population was ready for any path to peace, and soon one presented itself.

Rising almost mystically from the sheer chaos, the Taliban (derived from a Persian word meaning Islamic students or seekers), began to form under the leadership of a one-eyed cleric from Oruzgan province in central Afghanistan, who the world would come to know as Mullah Mohammad Omar. More as a result of timing than of military might, they swept through the Pashtun world of eastern Afghanistan, a welcome relief from the brigands controlling the valleys and mountain passes. By 1996 the Taliban had seized Kabul, and the Afghan people seemed to accept their deliverance. The West fleetingly saw the Taliban as the source of a new order and a possible tool in yet another replay of the Great Game—the race for the energy riches of Central Asia. U.S. and foreign oil firms were looking for ways to pipe the vast natural-gas reserves of Turkmenistan to energy-starved markets in Pakistan. By 1996, most of the route of the proposed pipeline was loosely under Taliban control, and the match of politics, power, and energy seemed attractive. But the optimism was short-lived. In 1997, plans for the Afghan pipeline were shelved and the country began an even sharper downward spiral, as the Taliban overreached in their quest to take control of the country. Their atrocious human rights record and treatment of women drew international scorn, and with the exception of diplomatic recognition from Saudi Arabia, the United Arab Emirates, and Pakistan, Afghanistan was in total isolation. Its failure as a state of any recognizable form was now complete.

Against this backdrop, the Afghan Arab troublemakers began to drift back to Afghanistan. Many of them, including Osama bin Ladin, had left Afghanistan after the Soviet defeat, full of determination to bring about radical societal change in their home countries. All failed, and many began roaming among the few remaining states in the world that served as safe havens for their kind, mostly behind the Iron Curtain. But with the collapse of the Soviet Union, the would-be terrorists of the world fell on hard times. They lost their playgrounds in Eastern Europe and the Soviet Union, and even the redoubtable Carlos pitched up in Khartoum—where, coincidentally, bin Ladin had also settled after a failed attempt to bring about change in his Saudi homeland. Bin Ladin engaged in a number of agricultural, construction, and business ventures, but most of his consciousness was consumed by a brooding hatred of the United States. This passion grew during the Gulf War, and five years later, with U.S. troops still stationed in Saudi Arabia, bin Ladin's rage found its final form. It would be the United States against which he would concentrate all of his energies.

By 1995, however, bin Ladin's presence in Sudan had become an issue both for the United States and for Saudi Arabia, which by this time had stripped bin Ladin of his Saudi citizenship. The Sudanese were quietly told that bin Ladin was a major obstacle to improved relations, and that Khartoum would be wise to ask him to leave. Sudan had already begun ridding itself of undesirables. In a dramatic setup, Carlos, stretched out on a Khartoum hospital operating table having a vasectomy reversed, was abruptly bundled up by French security officers and spirited off to Paris to stand trial for earlier crimes. According to a PBS Frontline television interview with Sudanese President Umar Hassan al-Bashir, the Sudanese government offered to keep bin Ladin on a tight leash, or even hand him over to the Saudis or the Americans. The Saudis reportedly declined the offer, for fear his presence would only cause more trouble in the royal kingdom, and the United States reportedly passed because it had no indictable complaints against bin Ladin at the time. In 1996, then, on U.S. and Saudi instructions, bin Ladin was expelled from Sudan, and he moved to the last stop on the terror line, Afghanistan. Still relatively unknown to the public, bin Ladin came into view through a CNN interview in 1997, when he claimed that his disciples had been behind the killing of 18 American soldiers in Somalia in 1993. The next year he issued a fatwa, an Islamic decree, of questionable authenticity, calling for all-out war against all Americans. But it was in August 1998 that he was indelibly etched into the world's consciousness, when terrorists thought to have links to his Al Qaeda organization struck simultaneously at American embassies in Kenya and Tanzania, killing 224 persons, including 12 Americans, and wounding 5,000. The U.S. response was quick but futile—75 cruise missiles were launched at bin Ladin's training camps in Afghanistan and at a pharmaceutical factory suspected of producing precursors for chemical weapons in Sudan. Bin Ladin escaped unharmed, and the attack on the Sudanese pharmaceutical factory remains a smoldering controversy to this day.

Back To The Future

Since 1998, the hunt for bin Ladin has been the driving force behind U.S. policy toward Afghanistan. Though the Taliban have repeatedly claimed that the Saudi has been under their control and incapable of fomenting the various attacks with which he is charged—including that against the U.S.S. Cole in Aden and those on the World Trade Center and the Pentagon—the U.S. government has little doubt that bin Ladin is the culprit. The confrontation with him and those who shelter him is at the point of no return.

It probably could not be otherwise, but how this first engagement in the new U.S. war on terrorism is conducted will be crucial to all that follows. The coalition being carefully constructed will function differently from that built for the Gulf War a decade ago. The bulk of the military tasks in that brief war against Iraq were intended from the outset to be carried out by the Americans, the British, and the French. The participation of the Arab states was not crucial to the fighting, though it was crucial to the U.S. ability to operate from bases near Iraq. In this new conflict, the roles will, in many ways, be reversed. The coalition partners from the Arab and Islamic states will have specific, front-line operational roles. They will serve as force multipliers for the usual alliance of American and European intelligence and security services and special operations forces. If the terror network is to be dismantled, it will be with help from the security services of Pakistan, Egypt, Jordan, Sudan, and a few others, not from the exclusive efforts of the United States or its European allies.

So the tale ends where it began, at Michni Point. As the Bush administration balances its military and political goals, plans to send U.S. troops into Afghanistan to seize bin Ladin should be weighed carefully for their practicality and political implications. Strident calls to add the overthrow of the Taliban regime to the list of American objectives may be attractive in terms of human rights, but that objective, too, must be weighed against the goal of making certain that the events of September 11 are not repeated.

Some have called for arming and forming an alliance with Afghanistan's now-leaderless Northern Alliance. This grouping of commanders, meticulously pulled together in shifting alliances by the late Ahmed Shah Masoud, now holds about ten percent of Afghan territory. Already the recipient of military and financial support from Russia and Iran, it seems a logical partner in the U.S. quest to locate and neutralize the bin Ladin network and replace the Taliban regime.

But that is not a wise course—not simply because of the cold irony of allying ourselves with the Russians in any fight in Afghanistan, but because it is not likely to achieve either goal. It is more than doubtful that the Northern Alliance forces could capture bin Ladin and his followers, and there is no reasonable guarantee that they could dislodge the Taliban. On the contrary, the more likely consequences of a U.S. alliance with the late Masoud's fighters would be the coalescing of Afghanistan's majority Pashtun tribes around their Taliban leaders and the rekindling of a brutal, general civil war that would continue until the United States simply gave up. The dominant tribe in Afghanistan, which also happens to be the largest, will dominate; replacing the Pashtun Taliban with the largely Tajik and Uzbek Northern Alliance is close to impossible. The threat of providing covert assistance to the Northern Alliance might be a useful short-term strategy to pressure the Taliban, if it is handled delicately, but any real military alliance to Masoud's successors will backfire.

The administration would do better to try to draw off segments of the Pashtun population only loosely allied with the Taliban regime. Those Pashtuns who signed on with the Taliban over the last five years did so because the Taliban seemed at the time to offer a fair chance for peace after decades of indescribably brutal war. They did not sign on to fight the United States, whose military might many of them will recall from the struggle against the Soviet occupation. The administration seems to realize this, and it is now moving quietly, gathering resources in the land of the Pashtun.

If anyone is to replace an emir in Afghanistan, it will have to be the people of Afghanistan themselves. Any doubters should ask the British and the Russians.

Osama Bin Laden: How the U.S. Helped Midwife a Terrorist

By Ahmed Rashid

In 1986, CIA chief William Casey had stepped up the war against the Soviet Union by taking three significant, but at that time highly secret, measures.

He had persuaded the US Congress to provide the Mujaheddin with American-made Stinger anti-aircraft missiles to shoot down Soviet planes and provide US advisers to train the guerrillas. Until then, no US-made weapons or personnel had been used directly in the war effort.

The CIA, Britain's MI6 and the ISI [Pakistan's Inter-Services Intelligence] also agreed on a provocative plan to launch guerrilla attacks into the Soviet Socialist Republics of Tajikistan and Uzbekistan, the soft Muslim underbelly of the Soviet state from where Soviet troops in Afghanistan received their supplies. The task was given to the ISI's favourite Mujaheddin leader, Gulbuddin Hikmetyar. In March 1987, small units crossed the Amu Darya river from bases in northern Afghanistan and launched their first rocket attacks against villages in Tajikistan. Casey was delighted with the news, and on his next secret trip to Pakistan he crossed the border into Afghanistan with [the late Pakistani] President Zia [ul-Haq] to review the Mujaheddin groups.

Thirdly, Casey committed CIA support to a long-standing ISI initiative to recruit radical Muslims from around the world to come to Pakistan and fight with the Afghan Mujaheddin. The ISI had encouraged this since 1982, and by now all the other players had their reasons for supporting the idea.

President Zia aimed to cement Islamic unity, turn Pakistan into the leader of the Muslim world and foster an Islamic opposition in Central Asia. Washington wanted to demonstrate that the entire Muslim world was fighting the Soviet Union alongside the Afghans and their American benefactors. And the Saudis saw an opportunity both to promote Wahabbism [their strict and austere creed] and to get rid of its disgruntled radicals. None of the players reckoned on these volunteers having their own agendas, which would eventually turn their hatred against the Soviets on their own regimes and the Americans.

Thousands of radicals come to study

...Between 1982 and 1992, some 35,000 Muslim radicals from 43 Islamic countries in the Middle East, North and East Africa, Central Asia and the Far East would pass their baptism under fire with the Afghan Mujaheddin. Tens of thousands more foreign Muslim radicals came to study in the hundreds of new madrassas that Zia's military government began to fund in Pakistan and along the Afghan border. Eventually more than 100,000 Muslim radicals were to have direct contact with Pakistan and Afghanistan and be influenced by the jihad.

In camps near Peshawar [near the Afghanistan border] and in Afghanistan, these radicals met each other for the first time and studied, trained and fought together. It was the first opportunity for most of them to learn about Islamic movements in other countries, and they forged tactical and ideological links that would serve them well in the future. The camps became virtual universities for future Islamic radicalism. None of the intelligence agencies involved wanted to consider the consequences of bringing together thousands of Islamic radicals from all over the world. "What was more important in the world view of history? The Taliban or the fall of the Soviet Empire? A few stirred-up Muslims or the liberation of Central Europe and the end of the Cold War?" said Zbigniew Brzezinski, a former US National Security Adviser. American citizens woke up to the consequences only when Afghanistan-trained Islamic militants blew up the World Trade Center in New York in 1993, killing six people and injuring 1,000.

"The war," wrote Samuel Huntington, "left behind an uneasy coalition of Islamist organizations intent on promoting Islam against all non-Muslim forces. It also left a legacy of expert and experienced fighters, training camps and logistical facilities, elaborate trans-Islam networks of personal and organization relationships, a substantial amount of military equipment including 300 to 500 unaccounted-for Stinger missiles, and, most important, a heady sense of power and self-confidence over what had been achieved and a driving desire to move on to other victories."

A young Bin Laden

…Among these thousands of foreign recruits was a young Saudi student, Osama Bin Laden, the son of a Yemeni construction magnate, Mohammed Bin Laden, who was a close friend of the late King Faisal and whose company had become fabulously wealthy on the contracts to renovate and expand the Holy Mosques of Mecca and Medina. The ISI had long wanted Prince Turki Bin Faisal, the head of Istakhbarat, the Saudi Intelligence Service, to provide a Royal Prince to lead the Saudi contingent in order to show Muslims the commitment of the Royal Family to the jihad. Only poorer Saudis, students, taxi drivers and Bedouin tribesmen had so far arrived to fight. But no pampered Saudi prince was ready to rough it out in the Afghan mountains. Bin Laden, although not a royal, was close enough to the royals and certainly wealthy enough to lead the Saudi contingent. Bin Laden, Prince Turki and [Lieutenant] General [Hameed] Gul [head of the ISI] were to become firm friends and allies in a common cause.

The centre for the Arab-Afghans [Filipino Moros, Uzbeks from Soviet Central Asia, Arabs from Algeria, Egypt, Saudi Arabia and Kuwait, and Uighurs from Xinjiang in China who had all come to fight with the Mujaheddin] was the offices of the World Muslim League and the Muslim Brotherhood in the northern Pakistan city of Peshawar. The centre was run by Abdullah Azam, a Jordanian Palestinian whom Bin Laden had first met at university in Jeddah and revered as his leader. Azam and his two sons were assassinated by a bomb blast in Peshawar in 1989.

During the 1980s, Azam had forged close links with Hikmetyar and Abdul Rasul Sayyaf, the Afghan Islamic scholar, whom the Saudis had sent to Peshawar to promote Wahabbism. Saudi funds flowed to Azam and the Makhtab at Khidmat or Services Center, which he created in 1984 to service the new recruits and receive donations from Islamic charities. Donations from Saudi Intelligence, the Saudi Red Crescent, the World Muslim League and private donations from Saudi princes and mosques were channelled through the Makhtab. A decade later, the Makhtab would emerge at the center of a web of radical organizations that helped carry out the World Trade Center bombing and the bombings of US embassies in Africa in 1998.

Until he arrived in Afghanistan, Bin Laden's life had hardly been marked by anything extraordinary. He was born around 1957, the 17th of 57 children sired by his Yemeni father and a Saudi mother, one of

Mohammed Bin Laden's many wives. Bin Laden studied for a master's degree in business administration at King Abdul Aziz University in Jeddah but soon switched to Islamic studies. Thin and tall, he is 6 feet 5 inches, with long limbs and a flowing beard. He towered above his contemporaries, who remember him as a quiet and pious individual but hardly marked out for greater things.

His father backed the Afghan struggle and helped fund it, so when Bin Laden decided to join up, his family responded enthusiastically. He first traveled to Peshawar in 1980 and met the Mujaheddin leaders, returning frequently with Saudi donations for the cause until 1982, when he decided to settle in Peshawar. He brought in his company engineers and heavy construction equipment to help build roads and depots for the Mujaheddin. In 1986, he helped build the Khost tunnel complex, which the CIA was funding as a major arms storage depot, training facility and medical center for the Mujaheddin, deep under the mountains close to the Pakistan border. For the first time in Khost he set up his own training camp for Arab Afghans, who now increasingly saw this lanky, wealthy and charismatic Saudi as their leader.

…Bin Laden later claimed to have taken part in ambushes against Soviet troops, but he mainly used his wealth and Saudi donations to build Mujaheddin projects and spread Wahabbism among the Afghans. After the death of Azam in 1989, he took over Azam's organization and set up Al Qaeda or Military Base as a service center for Arab-Afghans and their families and to forge a broad-based alliance among them. With the help of Bin Laden, several thousand Arab militants had established bases in the provinces of Kunar, Nuristan and Badakhshan, but their extreme Wahabbi practices made them intensely disliked by the majority of Afghans. Moreover, by allying themselves with the most extreme pro-Wahabbi Pashtun MuMeddin, the Arab-Afghans alienated the non-Pashtuns and the Shia Muslims.

Upset by U.S. role in Gulf War

…By 1990, Bin Laden was disillusioned by the internal bickering of the Mujaheddin and he returned to Saudi Arabia to work in the family business. He founded a welfare organization for Arab-Afghan veterans. Some 4,000 of them had settled in Mecca and Medina alone, and Bin Laden gave money to the families of those killed. After Iraq's invasion of Kuwait he lobbied the Royal Family to organize a popular defense of the kingdom and raise a force from the Afghan war veterans to fight

Iraq. Instead, King Fahd invited in the Americans. This came as an enormous shock to Bin Laden. As the 540,000 US troops began to arrive, Bin Laden openly criticized the Royal Family, lobbying the Saudi ulema [religious scholars] to issue fatwas, religious rulings, against non-Muslims being based in the country.

. . . In 1992, Bin Laden left for Sudan to take part in the Islamic revolution under way there under the charismatic Sudanese leader Hassan Turabi. Bin Laden's continued criticism of the Saudi Royal Family eventually annoyed them so much that they took the unprecedented step of revoking his citizenship in 1994. It was in Sudan, with his wealth and contacts, that Bin Laden gathered around him more veterans of the Afghan war, who were all disgusted by the American victory over Iraq and the attitude of the Arab ruling elites who allowed the US military to remain in the Gulf. As US and Saudi pressure mounted against Sudan for harboring Bin Laden, the Sudanese authorities asked him to leave.

In May 1996, Bin Laden travelled back to Afghanistan, arriving in Jalalabad in a chartered jet with an entourage of dozens of Arab militants, bodyguards and family members, including three wives and 13 children. Here he lived under the protection of the Jalalabad Shura [an advisory body or assembly], until the conquest of Kabul and Jalalabad by the Taliban in September 1996. In August 1996, he had issued his first declaration of jihad against the Americans, whom he said were occupying Saudi Arabia.

"The walls of oppression and humiliation cannot be demolished except in a rain of bullets," the declaration read. Striking up a friendship with [Taliban leader] Mullah [Mohammed] Omar, in 1997 he moved to Kandahar, Afghanistan, and came under the protection of the Taliban.

By now, the CIA had set up a special cell to monitor his activities and his links with other Islamic militants. A US State Department report in August 1996 noted that Bin Laden was "one of the most significant financial sponsors of Islamic extremist activities in the world." The report said that Bin Laden was financing terrorist camps in Somalia, Egypt, Sudan, Yemen...and Afghanistan. In April 1996, President Clinton signed the Anti-Terrorism Act, which allowed the US to block assets of terrorist organizations. It was first used to block Bin Laden's access to his fortune of an estimated US$250-300 million. A few months later, Egyptian intelligence declared that Bin Laden was training 1,000 militants, a second generation of Arab-Afghans, to bring about an Islamic revolution in Arab countries.

CIA tries snatch operation

In early 1997, the CIA constituted a squad that arrived in Peshawar to try to carry out a snatch operation to get Bin Laden out of Afghanistan. The Americans enlisted Afghans and Pakistanis to help them but aborted the operation. The US activity in Peshawar helped persuade Bin Laden to move to the safer confines of Kandahar. On 23 February 1998, at a meeting in the original Khost camp, all the groups associated with Al Qaeda issued a manifesto under the aegis of "The International Islamic Front for Jihad against Jews and Crusaders." The manifesto stated "for more than seven years the US has been occupying the lands of Islam in the holiest of places, the Arabian peninsular, plundering its riches, dictating to its rulers, humiliating its people, terrorizing its neighbours, and turning its bases in the peninsular into a spearhead through which to fight the neighbouring Muslim peoples."

The meeting issued a fatwa. "The ruling to kill the Americans and their allies—civilians and military—is an individual duty for every Muslim who can do it in any country in which it is possible to." Bin Laden had now formulated a policy that was not just aimed at the Saudi Royal Family or the Americans, but called for the liberation of the entire Muslim Middle East. As the American air war against Iraq escalated in 1998, Bin Laden called on all Muslims to "confront, fight and kill, Americans and Britons."

1998 U.S. Embassy bombings

However, it was the bombings in August 1998 of the US Embassies in Kenya and Tanzania that killed 220 people which made Bin Laden a household name in the Muslim world and the West. Just 13 days later, after accusing Bin Laden of perpetrating the attack, the USA retaliated by firing 70 cruise missiles against Bin Laden's camps around Khost and Jalalabad. Several camps which had been handed over by the Taliban to the Arab-Afghans and Pakistani radical groups were hit. The Al Badr camp controlled by Bin Laden and the Khalid bin Walid and Muawia camps run by the Pakistani Harakat ul Ansar were the main targets. Harakat used their camps to train militants for fighting Indian troops in Kashmir. Seven outsiders were killed in the strike—three

Yemenis, two Egyptians, one Saudi and one Turk. Also killed were seven Pakistanis and 20 Afghans.

In November 1998 the USA offered a US$5-million reward for Bin Laden's capture. The Americans were further galvanized when Bin Laden claimed that it was his Islamic duty to acquire chemical and nuclear weapons to use against the USA. "It would be a sin for Muslims not to try to possess the weapons that would prevent infidels from inflicting harm on Muslims. Hostility toward America is a religious duty and we hope to be rewarded for it by God," he said.

...After the Africa bombings, the US launched a truly global operation. More than 80 Islamic militants were arrested in a dozen different countries. Militants were picked up in a crescent running from Tanzania, Kenya, Sudan and Yemen to Pakistan, Bangladesh, Malaysia and the Phillipines."

In December 1998, Indian authorities detained Bangladeshi militants for plotting to bomb the US Consulate in Calcutta. Seven Afghan nationals using false Italian passports were arrested in Malaysia and accused of trying to start a bombing campaign." According to the FBI, militants in Yemen who kidnapped 16 Western tourists in December 1998 were funded by Bin Laden. In February 1999, Bangladeshi authorities said Bin Laden had sent US$1 million to the Harkat-ul-Jihad (HJ) in Dhaka, Bangladesh, some of whose members had trained and fought in Afghanistan. HJ leaders said they wanted to turn Bangladesh into a Taliban-style Islamic state.

Thousands of miles away in Nouakchott, the capital of Mauritania in West Africa, several militants were arrested who had also trained under Bin Laden in Afghanistan and were suspected of plotting bomb explosions. Meanwhile, during the trial of 107 Al-Jihad members at a military court in Cairo, Egyptian intelligence officers testified that Bin Laden had bankrolled Al-Jihad. In February 1999, the CIA claimed that through monitoring Bin Laden's communication network by satellite, they had prevented his supporters from carrying out seven bomb attacks against US overseas facilities in Saudi Arabia, Albania, Azerbaijan, Tajikistan, Uganda, Uruguay and the Ivory Coast—emphasizing the reach of the Afghan veterans.

...But it was Pakistan and Saudi Arabia, the original sponsors of the Arab-Afghans, who suffered the most as their activities rebounded. In March 1997, three Arab and two Tajik militants [from Tajikistan] were shot dead after a 36-hour gun battle between them and the police in an Afghan refugee camp near Peshawar. Belonging to the Wahabbi radical Tafkir group, they were planning to bomb an Islamic heads of state meeting in Islamabad.

Fighting in Kashmir against India

With the encouragement of Pakistan, the Taliban and Bin Laden, Arab-Afghans had enlisted in the Pakistani party Harkat-ut-Ansar to fight in Kashmir against Indian troops. By inducting Arabs who introduced Wahabbi-style rules in the Kashmir valley, genuine Kashmiri militants felt insulted. The US government had declared Ansar a terrorist organization in 1996 and it had subsequently changed its name to Harkat-ul-Mujaheddin. All the Pakistani victims of the US missile strikes on Khost belonged to Ansar. In 1999, Ansar said it would impose a strict Wahabbi-style dress code in the Kashmir valley and banned jeans and jackets. On 15 February 1999, they shot and wounded three Kashmiri cable television operators for relaying Western satellite broadcasts. Ansar had previously respected the liberal traditions of Kashmiri Muslims, but the activities of the Arab-Afghans hurt the legitimacy of the Kashmiri movement and gave India a propaganda coup.

Pakistan faced a problem when Washington urged Prime Minister Nawaz Sharif to help arrest Bin Laden. The ISI's close contacts with Bin Laden, and the fact that he was helping fund and train Kashmiri militants who were using the Khost camps, created a dilemma for Sharif when he visited Washington in December 1998. Sharif side-stepped the issue but other Pakistani officials were more brazen, reminding their American counterparts how they had both helped midwife Bin Laden in the 1980s and the Taliban in the 1990s. Bin Laden himself pointed to continued support from some elements in the Pakistani intelligence services in an interview. "As for Pakistan there are some governmental departments, which, by the Grace of God, respond to the Islamic sentiments of the masses in Pakistan. This is reflected in sympathy and co-operation. However, some other governmental departments fell into the trap of the infidels. We pray to God to return them to the right path," said Bin Laden.

Conundrums for Pakistan, Saudi Arabia

Support for Bin Laden by elements within the Pakistani establishment was another contradiction in Pakistan's Afghan policy....The US was Pakistan's closest ally, with deep links to the military and the ISI. But both the Taliban and Bin Laden provided sanctuary and training facilities for Kashmiri militants who were backed by Pakistan, and Islamabad had little interest in drying up that support. Even though the Americans repeatedly tried to persuade the ISI to cooperate in delivering Bin Laden, the ISI declined, although it did help the US arrest several of Bin Laden's supporters. Without Pakistan's support, the United States could not hope to launch a snatch by US commandos or more accurate bombing strikes, because it needed Pakistani territory to launch such raids. At the same time, the USA dared not expose Pakistan's support for the Taliban, because it still hoped for ISI cooperation in catching Bin Laden.

The Saudi conundrum was even worse. In July 1998 Prince Turki had visited Kandahar and a few weeks later 400 new pick-up trucks arrived in Kandahar for the Taliban, still bearing their Dubai license plates. The Saudis also gave cash for the Taliban's cheque book conquest of the north in the autumn. Until the Africa bombings and despite US pressure to end their support for the Taliban, the Saudis continued funding the Taliban and were silent on the need to extradite Bin Laden.

The truth about the Saudi silence was even more complicated. The Saudis preferred to leave Bin Laden alone in Afghanistan because his arrest and trial by the Americans could expose the deep relationship that Bin Laden continued to have with sympathetic members of the Royal Family and elements within Saudi intelligence, which could prove deeply embarrassing. The Saudis wanted Bin Laden either dead or a captive of the Taliban—they did not want him captured by the Americans.

...By now Bin Laden had developed considerable influence with the Taliban, but that had not always been the case. The Taliban's contact with the Arab-Afghans and their Pan-Islamic ideology was nonexistent until the Taliban captured Kabul in 1996. Pakistan was closely involved in introducing Bin Laden to the Taliban leaders in Kandahar, because it wanted to retain the Khost training camps for Kashmiri militants, which were now in Taliban hands. Persuasion by Pakistan, the Taliban's better-educated cadres, who also had Pan-Islamic ideas, and the lure of financial benefits from Bin Laden, encouraged the Taliban leaders to meet with Bin Laden and hand him back the Khost camps.

A life with the Taliban in Kandahar

Partly for his own safety and partly to keep control over him, the Taliban shifted Bin Laden to Kandahar in 1997. At first he lived as a paying guest. He built a house for Mullah Omar's family and provided funds to other Taliban leaders. He promised to pave the road from Kandahar airport to the city and build mosques, schools and dams, but his civic works never got started as his funds were frozen. While Bin Laden lived in enormous style in a huge mansion in Kandahar with his family, servants and fellow militants, the arrogant behaviour of the Arab-Afghans who arrived with him and their failure to fulfill any of their civic projects antagonized the local population. The Kandaharis saw the Taliban leaders as beneficiaries of Arab largesse rather than the people.

Bin Laden endeared himself further to the leadership by sending several hundred Arab-Afghans to participate in the 1997 and 1998 Taliban offensives in the north. These Wahabbi fighters helped the Taliban carry out massacres of the Shia Hazaras in the north. Several hundred Arab-Afghans, based in the Rishkor army garrison outside Kabul, fought on the Kabul front against [the Mujaheddin leader Ahmad Shah] Masud. Increasingly, Bin Laden's world view appeared to dominate the thinking of senior Taliban leaders. All-night conversations between Bin Laden and the Taliban leaders paid off. Until his arrival, the Taliban leadership had not been particularly antagonistic to the USA or the West but demanded recognition for their government. However, after the Africa bombings the Taliban became increasingly vociferous against the Americans, the UN, the Saudis and Muslim regimes around the world. Their statements increasingly reflected the language of defiance Bin Laden had adopted and which was not an original Taliban trait.

As US pressure on the Taliban to expel Bin Laden intensified, the Taliban said he was a guest and it was against Afghan tradition to expel guests. When it appeared that Washington was planning another military strike against Bin Laden, the Taliban tried to cut a deal with Washington—to allow him to leave the country in exchange for US recognition. Thus, until the winter of 1998 the Taliban saw Bin Laden as an asset, a bargaining chip over whom they could negotiate with the Americans.

The US State Department opened a satellite telephone connection to speak to Mullah Omar directly. The Afghanistan desk officers, helped by a Pushto translator, held lengthy conversations with Omar in which both sides explored various options, but to no avail. By early 1999 it began to dawn on the Taliban that no compromise with the US was possible and they began to see Bin Laden as a liability. A US deadline in February 1999 to the Taliban to either hand over Bin Laden or face the consequences forced the Taliban to make him disappear discreetly from Kandahar. The move bought the Taliban some time, but the issue was still nowhere near being resolved.

The Arab-Afghans had come full circle. From being mere appendages to the Afghan jihad and the Cold War in the 1980s they had taken centre stage for the Afghans, neighbouring countries and the West in the 1990s....Afghanistan was now truly a haven for Islamic internationalism and terrorism and the Americans and the West were at a loss as to how to handle it.

Osama Bin Laden: An Interview

In the first part of this interview which occurred in May 1998, a little over two months before the U.S. embassy bombings in Kenya and Tanzania, Osama bin Laden answers questions posed to him by some of his followers at his mountaintop camp in southern Afghanistan. In the latter part of the interview, ABC reporter John Miller is asking the questions.

...What is the meaning of your call for Muslims to take arms against America in particular, and what is the message that you wish to send to the West in general?

The call to wage war against America was made because America has spear-headed the crusade against the Islamic nation, sending tens of thousands of its troops to the land of the two Holy Mosques over and above its meddling in its affairs and its politics, and its support of the oppressive, corrupt and tyrannical regime that is in control. These are the reasons behind the singling out of America as a target. And not exempt of responsibility are those Western regimes whose presence in the region offers support to the American troops there. We know at least one reason behind the symbolic participation of the Western forces and that is to support the Jewish and Zionist plans for expansion of what is called the Great Israel. Surely, their presence is not out of concern over their interests in the region.... Their presence has no meaning save one and that is to offer support to the Jews in Palestine who are in need of their Christian brothers to achieve full control over the Arab Peninsula which they intend to make an important part of the so called Greater Israel....

There is an Arabic proverb that says "she accused me of having her malady, then snuck away." Besides, terrorism can be commendable and it can be reprehensible. Terrifying an innocent person and terrorizing him is objectionable and unjust, also unjustly terrorizing people is not right. Whereas, terrorizing oppressors and criminals and thieves and robbers is necessary for the safety of people and for the protection of their property. There is no doubt in this. Every state and every civilization and culture has to resort to terrorism under certain circumstances for the purpose of abolishing tyranny and corruption. Every country in the world has its own security system and its own security forces, its own police and its own army. They are all designed to terrorize whoever even contemplates to attack that country or its citizens. The terrorism we practice is of the commendable kind for it is directed at the tyrants and the aggressors and the enemies of Allah, the tyrants, the traitors who commit acts of treason against their own countries and their own faith and their own prophet and their own nation. Terrorizing those and punishing them are necessary measures to straighten things and to make them right. Tyrants and oppressors who subject the Arab nation to aggression ought to be punished. The wrongs and the crimes committed against the Muslim nation are far greater than can be covered by this interview. America heads the list of aggressors against Muslims. The recurrence of aggression against Muslims everywhere is proof enough. For over half a century, Muslims in Palestine have been slaughtered and assaulted and robbed of their honor and of their property. Their houses have been blasted, their crops destroyed. And the strange thing is that any act on their part to avenge themselves or to lift the injustice befalling them causes great agitation in the United Nations which hastens to call for an emergency meeting only to convict the victim and to censure the wronged and the tyrannized whose children have been killed and whose crops have been destroyed and whose farms have been pulverized....

In today's wars, there are no morals, and it is clear that mankind has descended to the lowest degrees of decadence and oppression. They rip us of our wealth and of our resources and of our oil. Our religion is under attack. They kill and murder our brothers. They compromise our honor and our dignity and dare we utter a single word of protest against the injustice, we are called terrorists. This is compounded injustice. And the United Nations insistence to convict the victims and support the aggressors constitutes a serious precedence which shows the extent of injustice that has been allowed to take root in this land....

What is your relationship with the Islamic movements in various regions of the world like Chechnya and Kashmir and other Arab countries?

Cooperation for the sake of truth and righteousness is demanded from Muslims. A Muslim should do his utmost to cooperate with his fellow Muslims. But Allah says of cooperation that it is not absolute for there is cooperation to do good, and there is cooperation to commit aggression and act unjustly. A Muslim is supposed to give his fellow Muslim guidance and support. He (Allah) said "Stand by your brother be he oppressor or oppressed." When asked how were they to stand by him if he were the oppressor, He answered them, saying "by giving him guidance and counsel." It all goes to say that Muslims should cooperate with one another and should be supportive of one another, and they should promote righteousness and mercy. They should all unite in the fight against polytheism and they should pool all their resources and their energy to fight the Americans and the Zionists and those with them. They should, however, avoid side fronts and rise over the small problems for these are less detrimental. Their fight should be directed against unbelief and unbelievers....

We heard your message to the American government and later your message to the European governments who participated in the occupation of the Gulf. Is it possible for you to address the people of these countries?

As we have already said, our call is the call of Islam that was revealed to Mohammed. It is a call to all mankind. We have been entrusted with good cause to follow in the footsteps of the Messenger and to communicate his message to all nations. It is an invitation that we extend to all the nations to embrace Islam, the religion that calls for justice, mercy and fraternity among all nations, not differentiating between black and white or between red and yellow except with respect to their devotedness. All people who worship Allah, not each other, are equal before Him. We are entrusted to spread this message and to extend that call to all the people. We, nonetheless, fight against their governments and all those who approve of the injustice they practice against us. We fight the governments that are bent on attacking our religion and on stealing our wealth and on hurting our feelings. And as I have mentioned before, we fight them, and those who are part of their rule are judged in the same manner....

In your last statement, there was a strong message to the American government in particular. What message do you have for the European governments and the West in general?

Praise be Allah and prayers and peace upon Mohammed. With respect to the Western governments that participated in the attack on the land of the two Holy Mosques regarding it as ownerless, and in the siege against the Muslim people of Iraq, we have nothing new to add to the previous message. What prompted us to address the American government in particular is the fact that it is on the head of the Western and the crusading forces in their fight against Islam and against Muslims. The two explosions that took place in Riyadh and in Khobar recently were but a clear and powerful signal to the governments of the countries which willingly participated in the aggression against our countries and our lives and our sacrosanct symbols. It might be beneficial to mention that some of those countries have begun to move towards independence from the American government with respect to the enmity that it continues to show towards the Muslim people. We only hope that they will continue to move in that direction, away from the oppressive forces that are fighting against our countries. We however, differentiate between the western government and the people of the West. If the people have elected those governments in the latest elections, it is because they have fallen prey to the Western media which portray things contrary to what they really are. And while the slogans raised by those regimes call for humanity, justice, and peace, the behavior of their governments is completely the opposite. It is not enough for their people to show pain when they see our children being killed in Israeli raids launched by American planes, nor does this serve the purpose. What they ought to do is change their governments which attack our countries. The hostility that America continues to express against the Muslim people has given rise to feelings of animosity on the part of Muslims against America and against the West in general. Those feelings of animosity have produced a change in the behavior of some crushed and subdued groups who, instead of fighting the Americans inside the Muslim countries, went on to fight them inside the United States of America itself.

The Western regimes and the government of the United States of America bear the blame for what might happen. If their people do not wish to be harmed inside their very own countries, they should seek to elect governments that are truly representative of them and that can protect their interests....

The enmity between us and the Jews goes far back in time and is deep rooted. There is no question that war between the two of us is inevitable. For this reason it is not in the interest of Western governments to expose the interests of their people to all kinds of retaliation for almost nothing. It is hoped that people of those countries will initiate a positive move and force their governments not to act on behalf of other states and other sects. This is what we have to say and we pray to Allah to preserve the nation of Islam and to help them drive their enemies out of their land.

American politicians have painted a distorted picture of Islam, of Muslims and of Islamic fighters. We would like you to give us the true picture that clarifies your viewpoint....

The leaders in America and in other countries as well have fallen victim to Jewish Zionist blackmail. They have mobilized their people against Islam and against Muslims. These are portrayed in such a manner as to drive people to rally against them. The truth is that the whole Muslim world is the victim of international terrorism, engineered by America at the United Nations. We are a nation whose sacred symbols have been looted and whose wealth and resources have been plundered. It is normal for us to react against the forces that invade our land and occupy it....

Quite a number of Muslim countries have seen the rise of militant movements whose purpose is to stand up in the face of the pressure exerted on the people by their own governments and other governments. Such as is the case in Egypt and Libya and North Africa and Algiers and such as was the case in Syria and in Yemen. There are also other militant groups currently engaged in the fight against the unbelievers and the crusaders as is the case in Kashmir and Chechnya and Bosnia and the African horn. Is there any message you wish to convey to our brothers who are fighting in various parts of the Islamic World?

…Tell the Muslims everywhere that the vanguards of the warriors who are fighting the enemies of Islam belong to them and the young fighters are their sons. Tell them that the nation is bent on fighting the enemies of Islam. Once again, I have to stress the necessity of focusing on the Americans and the Jews for they represent the spearhead with which the members of our religion have been slaughtered. Any effort directed against America and the Jews yields positive and direct results—Allah willing. It is far better for anyone to kill a single American soldier than to squander his efforts on other activities.…

John Miller's interview begins.

You come from a background of wealth and comfort to end up fighting on the front lines. Many Americans find that unusual.

This is difficult to understand, especially for him who does not understand the religion of Islam. In our religion, we believe that Allah has created us for the purpose of worshipping him. He is the one who has created us and who has favored us with this religion. Allah has ordered us to make holy wars and to fight to see to it that His word is the highest and the uppermost and that of the unbelievers the lowermost. We believe that this is the call we have to answer regardless of our financial capabilities. This too answers the claims of the West and of the secular people in the Arab world. They claim that this blessed awakening and the people reverting to Islam are due to economic factors. This is not so. It is rather a grace from Allah, a desire to embrace the religion of Allah. And this is not surprising. When the holy war called, thousands of young men from the Arab Peninsula and other countries answered the call and they came from wealthy backgrounds. Hundreds of them were killed in Afghanistan and in Bosnia and in Chechnya.

You have been described as the world's most wanted man, and there is word that the American government intends to put a price on your head—in the millions—when you are captured. Do you think they will do that? And does it bother you?

We do not care what the Americans believe. What we care for is to please Allah. Americans heap accusations on whoever stands for his religion or his rights or his wealth. It does not scare us that they have put a price on my head. We as Muslims believe that our years on this earth are finite and predetermined. If the whole world gets together to kill us before it is our time to go, they will not succeed. We also believe that livelihoods are preordained. So no matter how much pressure American puts on the regime in Riyadh to freeze our assets and to forbid people from contributing to this great cause, we shall still have Allah to take care of us; livelihood is sent by Allah; we shall not want.

Mr. bin Laden, you have issued a fatwah calling on Muslims to kill Americans where they can, when they can. Is that directed at all Americans, just the American military, just the Americans in Saudi Arabia?

Allah has ordered us to glorify the truth and to defend Muslim land, especially the Arab peninsula...against the unbelievers. After World War II, the Americans grew more unfair and more oppressive towards people in general and Muslims in particular.... The Americans started it and retaliation and punishment should be carried out following the principle of reciprocity, especially when women and children are involved. Through history, America has not been known to differentiate between the military and the civilians or between men and women or adults and children. Those who threw atomic bombs and used the weapons of mass destruction against Nagasaki and Hiroshima were the Americans. Can the bombs differentiate between military and women and infants and children? America has no religion that can deter her from exterminating whole peoples. Your position against Muslims in Palestine is despicable and disgraceful. America has no shame.... We believe that the worst thieves in the world today and the worst terrorists are the Americans. Nothing could stop you except perhaps retaliation in kind. We do not have to differentiate between military or civilian. As far as we are concerned, they are all targets, and this is what the fatwah says.... The fatwah is general (comprehensive) and it includes all those who participate in, or help the Jewish occupiers in killing Muslims.

Ramzi Yousef was a follower of yours. Do you remember him and did you know him?

After the explosion that took place in the World Trade Center, Ramzi Yousef became a well known Muslim figure. Muslims have come to know him. Unfortunately, I did not know him before this incident. I of course remember who he is. He is a Muslim who wanted to protect his religion jealously from the oppression practiced by America against Islam. He acted with zeal to make the Americans understand that their government was attacking Muslims in order to safeguard the American-Jewish interests.

Wali Khan Amin Shah was captured in Manila. American authorities believe he was working for you, funded by you, setting up training camps there and part of his plan was to plan out the assassination or the attempted assassination of President Clinton during his trip to Manila.

Wali Khan is a Muslim young man; his nickname in Afghanistan was the Lion. He was among the most courageous Muslim young men. He was a close friend and we used to fight from the same trenches in Afghanistan. We fought many battles against the Russians until they were defeated and put to shame and had to leave the country in disgrace. As to what you said about him working for me, I have nothing to say. We are all together in this; we all work for Allah and our reward comes from him. As to what you said about the attempt to assassinate President Clinton, it is not surprising. What do you expect from people attacked by Clinton, whose sons and mothers have been killed by Clinton? Do you expect anything but treatment by reciprocity?

The federal government in the US. is still investigating their suspicions that you ordered and funded the attack on the US military in Al Khobar and Riyadh.

We have roused the nation and the Muslim people and we have communicated to them the fatwahs of our learned scholars who the Saudi government has thrown in jail in order to please the American government for which they are agents.... We have communicated their fatwahs and stirred the nation to drive out the enemy who has occupied our land and usurped our country and suppressed our people and to rid the land of the two Holy Mosques from their presence. Among the young men who responded to our call are Khalid Al Said and Abdul Azeez Al...and Mahmud Al Hadi and Muslih Al Shamrani. We hope Allah receives them as holy martyrs. They have raised the nation's head high and washed away a great part of the shame that has enveloped us as a result of the weakness of the Saudi government and its complicity with the American government.... Yes, we have instigated and they have responded. We hope Allah grants their families solace.

You've been painted in America as a terrorist leader. To your follow-ers, you are a hero. How do you see yourself?

As I have said, we are not interested in what America says. We do not care. We view ourselves and our brothers like everyone else. Allah created us to worship Him and to follow in his footsteps and to be guided by His Book. I am one of the servants of Allah and I obey his orders. Among those is the order to fight for the word of Allah...and to fight until the Americans are driven out of all the Islamic countries.

No one expected the mujahedeen to beat the Russians in Afghanistan. It came as a surprise to everyone. What do you see as the future of American involvement in the Middle East, in taking on groups like this?

...Allah has granted the Muslim people and the Afghani mujahedeen, and those with them, the opportunity to fight the Russians and the So-viet Union.... They were defeated by Allah and were wiped out. There is a lesson here. The Soviet Union entered Afghanistan late in Decem-ber of '79. The flag of the Soviet Union was folded once and for all on the 25th of December just 10 years later. It was thrown in the waste basket. Gone was the Soviet union forever. We are certain that we shall—with the grace of Allah—prevail over the Americans and over the Jews, as the Messenger of Allah promised us in an authentic pro-phetic tradition when He said the Hour of Resurrection shall not come before Muslims fight Jews and before Jews hide behind trees and be-hind rocks.

We are certain—with the grace of Allah—that we shall prevail over the Jews and over those fighting with them. Today however, our battle against the Americans is far greater than our battle was against the Russians. Americans have committed unprecedented stupidity. They have attacked Islam and its most significant sacrosanct sym-bols.... We anticipate a black future for America. Instead of remaining United States, it shall end up separated states and shall have to carry the bodies of its sons back to America.

What do you see as the future of the Saudi royal family and their involvement with America and the US military?

History has the answer to your question. The fate of any government which sells the interests of its own people and, betrays the nation and commits offenses which furnish grounds for expulsion from Islam, is known. We expect for the ruler of Riyadh the same fate as the Shah of Iran. We anticipate this to happen to him and to the influential people who stand by him and who have sided with the Jews and the Christians giving them free reign over the land of the two Holy Mosques. These are grave offenses that are grounds for expulsion from the faith. They shall all be wiped out....

Describe the situation when your men took down the American forces in Somalia.

After our victory in Afghanistan and the defeat of the oppressors who had killed millions of Muslims, the legend about the invincibility of the superpowers vanished. Our boys no longer viewed America as a superpower. So, when they left Afghanistan, they went to Somalia and prepared themselves carefully for a long war. They had thought that the Americans were like the Russians, so they trained and prepared. They were stunned when they discovered how low was the morale of the American soldier. America had entered with 30,000 soldiers in addition to thousands of soldiers from different countries in the world.... As I said, our boys were shocked by the low morale of the American soldier and they realized that the American soldier was just a paper tiger. He was unable to endure the strikes that were dealt to his army, so he fled, and America had to stop all its bragging and all that noise it was making in the press after the Gulf War in which it destroyed the infrastructure and the milk and dairy industry that was vital for the infants and the children and the civilians and blew up dams which were necessary for the crops people grew to feed their families. Proud of this destruction, America assumed the titles of world leader and master of the new world order. After a few blows, it forgot all about those titles and rushed out of Somalia in shame and disgrace, dragging the bodies of its soldiers. America stopped calling itself world leader and master of the new world order, and its politicians realized that those titles were too big for them and that they were unworthy of them. I was in Sudan when this happened. I was very happy to learn of that great defeat that America suffered, so was every Muslim....

Many Americans believe that fighting army to army like what happened in Afghanistan is heroic for either army. But sending off bombs, killing civilians like in the World Trade Center is terrorism.

...After our victory over the Russians in Afghanistan, the international and the American mass media conducted fierce campaigns against us... They called us terrorists even before the mujahedeen had committed any act of terrorism against the real terrorists who are the Americans. On the other hand, we say that American politics and their religion do not believe in differentiating between civilians and military, between infants and animals, or among any human groups....

Our mothers and daughters and sons are slaughtered every day with the approval of America and its support. And, while America blocks the entry of weapons into Islamic countries, it provides the Israelis with a continuous supply of arms allowing them thus to kill and massacre more Muslims. Your religion does not forbid you from committing such acts, so you have no right to object to any response or retaliation that reciprocates your own actions. But, and in spite of this, our retaliation is directed primarily against the soldiers only and against those standing by them. Our religion forbids us from killing innocent people such as women and children. This, however, does not apply to women fighters. A woman who puts herself in the same trench with men, gets what they get....

The American people, by and large, do not know the name bin Laden, but they soon likely will. Do you have a message for the American people?

I say to them that they have put themselves at the mercy of a disloyal government, and this is most evident in Clinton's administration.... We believe that this administration represents Israel inside America. Take the sensitive ministries such as the Ministry of Exterior and the Ministry of Defense and the CIA, you will find that the Jews have the upper hand in them. They make use of America to further their plans for the world, especially the Islamic world. American presence in the Gulf provides support to the Jews and protects their rear. And while millions of Americans are homeless and destitute and live in abject poverty, their government is busy occupying our land and building new settlements and helping Israel build new settlements in the point of departure for our Prophet's midnight journey to the seven heavens. America throws her own sons in the land of the two Holy Mosques for the sake of protecting Jewish interests....

The American government is leading the country towards hell.... We say to the Americans as people and to American mothers, if they cherish their lives and if they cherish their sons, they must elect an American patriotic government that caters to their interests not the interests of the Jews. If the present injustice continues with the wave of national consciousness, it will inevitably move the battle to American soil, just as Ramzi Yousef and others have done. This is my message to the American people. I urge them to find a serious administration that acts in their interest and does not attack people and violate their honor and pilfer their wealth....

In America, we have a figure from history from 1897 named Teddy Roosevelt. He was a wealthy man, who grew up in a privileged situation and who fought on the front lines. He put together his own men— hand chose them—and went to battle. You are like the Middle East version of Teddy Roosevelt.

I am one of the servants of Allah. We do our duty of fighting for the sake of the religion of Allah. It is also our duty to send a call to all the people of the world to enjoy this great light and to embrace Islam and experience the happiness in Islam. Our primary mission is nothing but the furthering of this religion.... Let not the West be taken in by those who say that Muslims choose nothing but slaughtering. Their brothers in East Europe, in Turkey and in Albania have been guided by Allah to submit to Islam and to experience the bliss of Islam. Unlike those, the European and the American people and some of the Arabs are under the influence of Jewish media....

Buried Alive
Afghan Women Under the Taliban
By Jan Goodwin

February 27, 1998—Thirty-thousand men and boys poured into the dilapidated Olympic sports stadium in Kabul, capital of Afghanistan. Street hawkers peddled nuts, biscuits and tea to the waiting crowd. The scheduled entertainment? They were there to see a young woman, Sohaila, receive 100 lashes, and to watch two thieves have their right hands amputated. Sohaila had been arrested walking with a man who was not a relative, a sufficient crime for her to be found guilty of adultery. Since she was single, it was punishable by flogging; had she been married, she would have been publicly stoned to death.

As Sohaila, completely covered in the shroud-like *burqa* veil, was forced to kneel and then flogged, Taliban "cheerleaders" had the stadium ringing with the chants of onlookers. Among those present there were just three women: the young Afghan, and two female relatives who had accompanied her. The crowd fell silent only when the luckless thieves were driven into the arena and pushed to the ground. Physicians using surgical scalpels promptly carried out the amputations. Holding the severed hands aloft by the index fingers, a grinning Taliban fighter warned the huge crowd, "These are the chopped-off hands of thieves, the punishment for any of you caught stealing." Then, to restore the party atmosphere, the thieves were driven in a jeep once around the stadium, a flourish that brought the crowd to their feet, as was intended.

These Friday circuses, at which Rome's Caligula would doubtless have felt at home, are to become weekly fixtures for the entertainment-starved male residents of Kabul. Now that "weak officials" have been purged from key ministries, says the city's governor, Manan Niazi, who like many of the regime's officials is also a mullah, the way has been cleared for such displays. "We have a lot of such unpunished cases, but the previous civil servants didn't have the courage to do what we are doing. These people have now been replaced, and these events will continue." In fact, the next scheduled program, as announced, would be one stoning to death and three amputations.

Earlier that same week, three men accused of "buggery" had been sentenced to death by being partially buried in the ground and then having a wall pushed over on them by a bulldozer, a bizarre and labor-intensive form of execution dreamed up by the supreme leader of the Taliban, the 36-year-old Mullah Mohammad Omar. After another man, a saboteur, was hanged, his corpse was driven around the city, swinging from a crane. Clearly, there is nothing covert about the regime's punitive measures. In fact, the Taliban insure they are as widely publicized as possible. Last March, for example, the regime's radio station, the only one permitted to operate, broadcast to the nation that a young woman caught trying to flee Afghanistan with a man who was not her relative had been stoned to death. On another occasion, it was announced over the airwaves that 225 women had been rounded up and sentenced to a lashing for violating the dress code. One woman had the top of her thumb amputated for the crime of wearing nail polish. And when the Taliban castrated and then hanged the former communist president and his brother in 1996, they left their bloodied bodies dangling from lampposts in busy downtown Kabul for three days. Photographs of the corpses appeared in news magazines and newspapers around the world.

The Taliban now control between 65 and 85 percent of Afghanistan, a country where statistics are anyone's guess. (Even the population size of Afghanistan is uncertain: possibly 15, maybe 22 million. The U.S. Department of State's figure on war fatalities—1.5 million—has not changed since 1985, although the armed conflict there is now in its 19th year.) For the last two years, the Taliban have been trying to win both a seat at the United Nations and international recognition. Thus far, only three countries have recognized the regime: Pakistan, the United Arab Emirates, and Saudi Arabia. And even Pakistan is becoming embarrassed by its neighbor.

Until the Taliban came to power, Saudi Arabia was the most oppressive country on earth for women, and many of the Taliban's restrictions are rooted in that hardline Gulf state's gender apartheid. Saudi Arabia has also been financially supportive of the Taliban and the religious schools in which they are indoctrinated. "We have long regarded the Saudi kingdom as our right hand," says the head of the Taliban governing council.

The Taliban regime claim they are restoring Afghanistan to the "purity of Islam," and the Western press invariably parrots them. But authorities in a number of Muslim countries insist that few of the regime's dictates have a basis in Islam. And just as the U.N. has denied the Taliban a seat in the General Assembly, so too, the Organization of Islamic Conference, a 55-country body, has withheld both a seat and recognition from the regime. "The Taliban is not the image the Islamic world wants to project," says one Muslim diplomat. And with good reason.

Now in its fourth year of existence, the pariah regime has expunged all leisure activities. Their list of what is illegal grows daily: music, movies and television, picnics, wedding parties, New Year celebrations, any kind of mixed-sex gathering. They've also banned children's toys, including dolls and kites; card and board games; cameras; photographs and paintings of people and animals; pet parakeets; cigarettes and alcohol; magazines and newspapers, and most books. They've even forbidden applause—a moot point, since there's nothing left to applaud.

"Whatever we are doing in our country, it is not in order for the world to be happy with us," Sher Abbas Stanakzai, who until recently was the Taliban's 36-year-old deputy Minister of Foreign Affairs, told me during my visit. Explaining why his regime has banned virtually all forms of entertainment, he says, "Time should be spent serving the country and praying to God. Nothing else. Everything else is a waste of time, and people are not allowed to waste their time."

For women, the restrictions are even harsher. Female education, from kindergarten through graduate school, banned. Employment for women, banned. It's now illegal to wear makeup, nail polish, jewelry, pluck your eyebrows, cut your hair short, wear colorful or stylish clothes, sheer stockings, white socks and shoes, high-heel shoes, walk loudly, talk loudly or laugh in public. In fact, the government doesn't believe women should go out at all: "Women, you should not step outside your residence" reads one of the Taliban dictates.

If women do venture out, it must be for an essential, government-sanctioned purpose, and they must wear the all-enveloping burqa. Even then they risk their lives. Not so long ago, a young mother, Torpeka, was shot repeatedly by the Taliban while rushing her seriously ill toddler to a doctor. Veiled as the law requires, she was spotted by a teenage Taliban guard, who tried to stop her because she shouldn't have left her home. Afraid her child might die if she were delayed, Torpeka kept going. The guard aimed his Kalashnikov machine-gun and fired several rounds directly at her. She was hit, but didn't die on the spot, as she could have. Instead, Afghans watching the incident in the crowded marketplace intervened, and Torpeka and her child received prompt medical attention. When her family later complained to the Taliban authorities, they were informed that it was the injured woman's fault. She had no right being out in public in the first place.

The *burqa* is a garment that covers women from head to toe, the heavy gauze patch across the eyes makes it hard to see, and completely blocks peripheral vision. Since enforced veiling, a growing number of women have been hit by vehicles because the burqa leaves them unable to walk fast, or see where they are going. Recently in Kabul, a Taliban tank rolled right over a veiled woman. Fortunately, she fell between the tracks. Instead of being crushed to death, she was not seriously hurt, but was severely traumatized.

To insure women are effaced as effectively as if they never existed, the government ordered all exterior windows of homes to be painted black. The only public transport permitted women are special buses, which are rarely available, and have all windows, except the driver's, covered with thick blankets.

It is now illegal for women to talk to any men except close relatives, which precludes them from visiting male physicians, no matter how sick. At the time of my recent visit, the evening curfew began at 7:30 p.m., after which no one, except government troops, was allowed out, even for medical emergencies. Even women in labor and needing hospital care must remain at home until morning.

It would probably be quicker to list what the Taliban haven't banned. The regime has even outlawed paper bags. Like many of their edicts, this would be laughable if the penalties for infractions weren't so severe. Break the Taliban's law and you risk imprisonment, flogging, or worse. And to insure their dictates are followed, religious police, part of the "Department for the Propagation of Virtue and the Suppression of Vice," constantly roam the streets. Often teenage boys armed with automatic weapons, they also carry broken-off car aerials or electrical cabling to whip women they decide are not properly observing the regulations.

Despite its disastrous and very public record on human rights, when the Taliban was petitioning the United Nations for a seat in the General Assembly last May, its then New York representative, Abdul Hakeem Mujahid, claimed his government was "protecting human rights and liberties in Afghanistan." He also stated that, having put a stop to the "miserable living conditions under which our women were living," they had "restored women's safety, dignity and freedom." He then went on to justify the Taliban's ban on women's education: Afghanistan lacks the resources to educate them, he said, adding that the Taliban also do not trust the values that became part of the education system under previous governments. Those reservations, however, only apply to women, since the regime continues to educate boys.

Mujahid omitted to mention a personal detail—how he circumvents the ban for his own daughter by sending her to an English-language school in Pakistan. But this kind of hypocrisy is common in Afghanistan today. Under the regime, cigarette smoking is severely punished, yet in every Taliban office I entered in Kabul, even that of the head of the department of Virtue and Vice, Mullah Qalam-ad-Din, from whom most of the restrictions originate, used ashtrays were always in evidence. A senior official in the foreign ministry chain-smoked throughout our hour-long conversation. "Isn't that illegal?" I asked. "I can't help it, I'm addicted," he replied with a smile.

While touting to the U.N. the Taliban's "improved" living conditions for women, Mujahid didn't mention the regime's banning of women's employment, or any of their myriad other restrictions, which have so constrained women's lives that half the population of the country is now effectively confined to house arrest.

Amnesty International calls Afghanistan under the Taliban "a human rights catastrophe." Afghan women, struggling to survive in what has become a police state claiming to be a theocracy, describe themselves as the "living dead."

It is hardly surprising, then, that the U.N. has not seated the Taliban delegation; or, indeed, that the credentials committee has refused even to meet with the regime's representative in New York, and most officials prefer to duck his phone calls. But the U.N. has seated the representatives of some pretty brutal regimes in the past, and the ostracism is unlikely to last forever—especially with lobbyists for American oil concerns entering the picture.

Unocal, a California-based global energy company, heads up one of two consortiums engaged in fierce competition to build gas and oil pipelines from landlocked Turkmenistan to Pakistan through war-torn Afghanistan. In testimony to the U.S. Congress this February, John Maresca, vice-president in charge of Unocal's international relations, referred to the $4.5 billion, some 790-mile project as the "new Silk

Road...a commercial corridor that can link Central Asia supply with the demand, once again making Central Asia the crossroads between Europe and Asia."

Iran offers an alternative pipeline route, but because of U.S. sanctions legislation, American companies would not be able to participate in its construction-or, as a result, gain any benefit from what are considered the largest untapped oil and gas reserves outside the Middle East. And while Unocal says it cannot sign any deal with the Taliban until they are formally recognized, this hasn't stopped them from wining and dining Taliban officials, and arranging shopping trips for them to purchase luxury items on their visits to the oil company in the U.S. Unocal already has a $900,000 training program underway, in collaboration with the University of Nebraska at Omaha, for pipeline construction personnel, a program limited to Afghan males. Additionally, the duo has established two technician training centers in Afghanistan, also benefitting men only.

Unocal's main partner in the consortium is Delta Oil Co., a Saudi-owned company, in whose behalf former White House legislative assistant Paul Behrends and Delta's American vice-president Charles Santos, a recent U.N. peace negotiator in Afghanistan, are busy lobbying in Washington.

The pipeline would bring the Taliban some $100 million annually in transit fees, in addition to providing thousands of jobs and improving infrastructure—building roads, supplying electricity, telephones, etc.—in the war-devastated country. The Clinton administration reportedly supports the Afghan pipeline, which would free the new nations of Central Asia from dependence on Russia, avoid the Iranian route, and bring needed energy to the Indian subcontinent.

Competing with Unocal to build the pipeline is Bridas International of Argentina, whose managing director, Mario Lopez Olacireegui, has gone on record saying he is not concerned about the Taliban's human rights violations. "We are just an oil and gas company," he says. "We are not bothered by human rights or politics." The Taliban, for their part, say they will award the pipeline contract to the consortium that is first able to start construction. Unocal's deadline to begin is this coming December.

A number of American women's organizations, headed by the Feminist Majority and the National Organization for Women, have mobilized to prevent the Clinton administration from recognizing the Taliban government unless it radically changes its treatment of women.

They are also campaigning for Unocal to include women in their training programs. As we went to press, sources within Unocal admitted this campaign is beginning to have an effect. A split has occurred within the oil company—those who want to press ahead, and those who do not want a politically embarrassing "rogue operation." As the U.S. women's campaign gains momentum, Unocal is also finding foreign investors suddenly unenthusiastic about being affiliated with a regime with such a disastrous public relations record. None of which has affected the Taliban, however, who have since clamped down harder on women, this time ordering that all foreign Muslim women working with the U.N. or NGOs be accompanied by male chaperones, which in effect will halt their employment in Afghanistan.

While it may be some time before Taliban coffers are swollen by petrodollars, one of the mainstays of the regime's economy is heroin production, which they use in part to supply their war machine. Afghanistan now produces more of the narcotic than any other country—and much of it ends up on the streets of the U.S. Despite promises by the Taliban to eradicate the industry, according to a report released last February by the U.N. International Narcotics Control Board, the harvest of opium poppy, from which heroin is derived, increased by 25 percent in Afghanistan during 1997. The Taliban control 96 percent of Afghanistan's total opium output, this country's only real remaining cash crop.

Though it was always impoverished, before the Soviet invasion Afghanistan was able to feed its people. Today, after almost 20 years of war, this is no longer true. Afghan women, in the rural areas, have always worked alongside men in the fields. In the capital, until the Taliban took over, they often wore Western dress, served in parliament, and worked in a variety of professions, including medicine, engineering, architecture, the media and law. During the long years of fighting, as men were killed, went missing, or became disabled, the survival of many families came to depend on women's income.

Before the Taliban ban on female employment, 70 percent of the teachers in Kabul were women, as were 50 percent of the civil servants and university students, and 40 percent of the doctors.

Why does the regime insist that women be confined at home? Reducing women to mere objects, the minister of education says, "It's like having a flower, or a rose. You water it and keep it at home for yourself, to look at it and smell it. It [a woman] is not supposed to be taken out of the house to be smelled." Another Taliban leader is less poetic:

"There are only two places for Afghan women—in her husband's house, and in the graveyard."

I have been visiting and reporting on Afghanistan since 1984, and have traveled extensively throughout the country, but it was only during my visit last fall that I saw for the first time legions of women and children reduced to beggary, the result of the Taliban's ban on women's employment. Many families, having sold all their household items, even blankets, are surviving on bread and sugarless tea. Supplementary feeding centers, funded by foreign agencies, are dotted across the capital. Here, malnourished children—four-year-olds weighing 16 pounds, 18-month-old toddlers weighing 9 pounds—are fed. Their mothers are not, even though they, too, are malnourished. Women often eat once every two or three days, preferring instead to give whatever food they have to their children. According to new U.N. figures, some 40 percent of the Kabul population now exists on food handouts, either from humanitarian agencies or from begging.

The legally mandated *burqa* has also become a severe financial hardship. The veil now costs the equivalent of five months salary—if any women were still receiving one. Most cannot afford to buy the garment, and whole neighborhoods must share one. It can take several days for a woman's turn to come round; even if she has money to shop for food, she can't go out until then.

In Kabul, the number of street children has risen from an estimated 28,000 to 60,000 in the last year. This city, once a symbol of modernity for Afghanistan, is now in ruins—the most bomb-damaged capital in the world. It is also the most land-mined. Mines maim and/or kill an average of 25 people a day in Afghanistan. Two-thirds of them are children. It is predominantly children who herd animals, or search for fuel or for scrap metal to sell to help support their families. Scrap metal merchants will only purchase unexploded bombs or shells if the children disarm them first. Kids doing this highly risky work earn on average enough to buy just two or three pieces of bread per day.

Despite the terrible toll mines are taking, the Taliban have interfered with programs to teach women and children how to locate and stay clear of mines. Board games used by foreign humanitarian agencies to instruct a mostly illiterate population in mine-awareness have been disallowed because they use now-banned pictures of humans or animals coming too close to a mine; an alternative, flash cards, has also been outlawed—as gambling.

Conditions are so deplorable for women under the Taliban that many are now severely depressed. Without the resources to leave the country, an increasing number are now choosing suicide, once rare there, as a means of escape. A European physician working in the city told me, "Doctors are seeing a lot of esophageal burns. Women are swallowing battery acid, or poisonous household cleansers, because they are easy to find. But it's a very painful way to die."

Spoghmai, a 24-year-old former teacher, refers to herself as being "buried alive." The young woman lost her right arm up to the shoulder, and her right leg to the thigh, in a shelling attack three years ago. After her injury, when she spent weeks in a poorly equipped hospital, Spoghmai was, not surprisingly, so depressed she wanted to die. A life-saver, literally, was a job she found with a Western relief agency that enabled her to work with the disabled. But four months later, when the Taliban took Kabul in September 1996, she was forced to stop working.

Today, she wears a badly fitted, and painful, prosthesis—badly fitted because, in Afghanistan now, false limbs come in only three sizes. Disabled as she is, walking is difficult, and is impossible if she is wearing a burqa veil. Since she cannot go out without one, she hasn't left the house in two years. "There are so many days when I am too depressed to get out of bed. Why should I? There is nothing for me to do. So many times I ask, Why didn't I die when I was injured?"

I offered to take Spoghmai out for a short excursion in my jeep. She refused. "I am afraid. It is too dangerous, for you and me. Afghans are not allowed to be with foreigners, or talk with journalists. If we are caught, the Taliban will beat us, maybe worse. And anyway, to go out briefly would be too painful. It will remind me of what I have lost. One day of freedom will make this prison so much worse."

International Complicity

A major concern today is how most of the international community operating in Afghanistan is going along with the Taliban's restrictions on women out of fear of having their agencies forced to close. Complicating this issue is the fact that a number of U.N. officials posted there in senior positions are from developing countries where women are traditionally second class. Consequently, they consider the Taliban's restrictions on women unimportant, or choose to look the other way. One such head of a U.N. agency in Kabul has often told colleagues, "the gender issue is too dangerous, I don't plan to risk my career over it."

The director of a major American humanitarian agency in Kabul, who asked that his name not be used for security reasons, admitted he found it "personally abhorrent," but felt he had no choice when he had to tell his female employees first to wear the burqa, and then to stay home. "I felt awful that I was forcing them to veil. When you only see women in burqas, you realize the power of covering a woman like that. You don't treat them like people anymore, just bits of cloth moving down the street. But on a pragmatic level, that's what had to happen to keep everybody safe, and to keep our program moving.

"When the Taliban started threatening and then beating our guards and drivers, we had no choice. When I realized that no one, no authority, was going to stop the Taliban from beating women if they worked, it became an issue of protecting the staff. I know that is a rationalization, but they have demonstrated what the consequences are of not complying with their edicts. And so you compromise."

He admits that there is an "incredible drift in the international community here with regard to the gender issue. Women are told: 'Stay home, suffer your fate, it's easier for everyone.' It's a slippery slope we're on."

One agency in Kabul, Oxfam, which is headed by a retired American professor, Nancy Smith, chose to make a stand against the regime, and closed down her multimillion-dollar program until such time as the Taliban remove the restrictions on women. With her agency charged with restoring 40 percent of the water supply system to Kabul, a project that would also benefit the Taliban, Smith, a wiry 65-year-old, told the regime her agency's mandate was to relieve poverty, distress and suffering, and that included women's. "We concluded that our core principles are not negotiable," she says. "Oxfam will work with women in Kabul, or not at all."

Afghan women also defy the Taliban. I visited several underground schools that women were running for girls out of their homes. Operating one-room school houses accommodating students aged six to 24, these dedicated women were breaking the Taliban law on a number of counts, including the one forbidding gatherings of unrelated people. In a city where paper and pencils are now hard to acquire, the teaching aids were handmade from scraps of whatever they could find, including stones and twigs.

While these women risk their safety to keep teaching, much of the regime that threatens them are either illiterate or nearly so. Even the Taliban's Ministers of Education and Higher Education have little schooling. Most Talibs (the name means religious student) are young zealots, graduates of the regime's madrassas, so-called religious schools that are based, for the most part, in Pakistan, and funded in part by the Saudis. In these cloister-like environments, boys grow up totally segregated from any women, including those in their own families. The highest honor they can earn there is that of qari, a Muslim honorific given to those who memorize and can recite the entire Koran, and a number do. Sadly, however, they learn to do so in Arabic, a language they do not understand, and is not taught to them. Consequently, they have no idea of the rights given to women in Islam.

"Islam dictates that education is mandatory for both males and females," says Zieba Shorish-Shamley, Ph.D., chair of the Women's Alliance for Peace and Human Rights in Afghanistan, based in Washington, D.C. Hassan Hathout, M.D., Ph.D., the director of the outreach program at the Islamic Center of Southern California, agrees: "At the time of the Prophet, Muslim women attained such scholarship they became teachers to prominent men." They also worked. In fact, the Prophet met his first wife because she was his employer. "The medical corps of the Prophet's army was an all-woman corps, and in some battles, women took up swords and joined active combat. Women participated in public affairs, were involved in negotiating treaties, were even judges. Islam declared gender equality through the Prophet's words, 'Women are the siblings of men.'"

Islamic scriptures are very clear on the veil: Only the prophet's wives were required to cover their faces. In fact, when women undertake the Islamic pilgrimage to Mecca, the Hajj, they are required to do so with their faces uncovered. They also mingle with men not related to them.

"Obviously, the Taliban's military prowess far exceeds their knowledge of Islam," says Dr. Hathout. Perhaps the regime's most important oversight is the Prophet Mohammad's teaching: "There is no compulsion in Islam."

When I raised these issues with the chief mullah of the Department of Virtue and Vice, and asked him why, if such things were good enough for the Prophet, they weren't good enough for the Taliban, he grinned and changed the subject. The regime's Sher Abbas Stanakzai was more honest when he admitted, "Our current restrictions are necessary in order to bring the Afghan people under control. We need these restrictions until people learn to obey the government."

Jihad vs. McWorld

By Benjamin R. Barber

The two axial principles of our age—tribalism and global-ism—clash at every point except one: they may both be threatening to democracy

Just beyond the horizon of current events lie two possible political fu-tures—both bleak, neither democratic. The first is a retribalization of large swaths of humankind by war and bloodshed: a threatened Leba-nonization of national states in which culture is pitted against culture, people against people, tribe against tribe—a Jihad in the name of a hundred narrowly conceived faiths against every kind of interdepend-ence, every kind of artificial social cooperation and civic mutuality. The second is being borne in on us by the onrush of economic and eco-logical forces that demand integration and uniformity and that mesmer-ize the world with fast music, fast computers, and fast food—with MTV, Macintosh, and McDonald's, pressing nations into one commer-cially homogenous global network: one McWorld tied together by technology, ecology, communications, and commerce. The planet is falling precipitantly apart *AND* coming reluctantly together at the very same moment.

These two tendencies are sometimes visible in the same countries at the same instant: thus Yugoslavia, clamoring just recently to join the New Europe, is exploding into fragments; India is trying to live up to its reputation as the world's largest integral democracy while powerful new fundamentalist parties like the Hindu nationalist Bharatiya Janata Party, along with nationalist assassins, are imperiling its hard-won unity. States are breaking up or joining up: the Soviet Union has disap-peared almost overnight, its parts forming new unions with one another or with like-minded nationalities in neighboring states. The old inter-

Published originally in The Atlantic Monthly, March 1992 as an introduction to *Jihad vs. McWorld* (Ballantine paperback, 1996), a volume that discusses and extends the themes of the original article "Benjamin R. Barber *Jihad Vs. McWorld*" by Benjamin R. Barber in this textbook. Copyright © 1992, Benja-min R. Barber. All rights reserved. The Atlantic Monthly, March 1992, vol-ume 269, No. 3 pages 53-65.

war national state based on territory and political sovereignty looks to be a mere transitional development.

The tendencies of what I am here calling the forces of Jihad and the forces of McWorld operate with equal strength in opposite directions, the one driven by parochial hatreds, the other by universalizing markets, the one re-creating ancient subnational and ethnic borders from within, the other making national borders porous from without. They have one thing in common: neither offers much hope to citizens looking for practical ways to govern themselves democratically. If the global future is to pit Jihad's centrifugal whirlwind against McWorld's centripetal black hole, the outcome is unlikely to be democratic—or so I will argue.

McWorld, or the Globalization of Politics

Four imperatives make up the dynamic of McWorld: a market imperative, a resource imperative, an information-technology imperative, and an ecological imperative. By shrinking the world and diminishing the salience of national borders, these imperatives have in combination achieved a considerable victory over factiousness and particularism, and not least of all over their most virulent traditional form—nationalism. It is the realists who are now Europeans, the utopians who dream nostalgically of a resurgent England or Germany, perhaps even a resurgent Wales or Saxony. Yesterday's wishful cry for one world has yielded to the reality of McWorld.

THE MARKET IMPERATIVE. Marxist and Leninist theories of imperialism assumed that the quest for ever-expanding markets would in time compel nation-based capitalist economies to push against national boundaries in search of an international economic imperium. Whatever else has happened to the scientist predictions of Marxism, in this domain they have proved farsighted. All national economies are now vulnerable to the inroads of larger, transnational markets within which trade is free, currencies are convertible, access to banking is open, and contracts are enforceable under law. In Europe, Asia, Africa, the South Pacific, and the Americas such markets are eroding national sovereignty and giving rise to entities—international banks, trade associations, transnational lobbies like OPEC and Greenpeace, world news services like CNN and the BBC, and multinational corporations that increasingly lack a meaningful national identity—that neither reflect nor respect nationhood as an organizing or regulative principle.

The market imperative has also reinforced the quest for international peace and stability, requisites of an efficient international economy. Markets are enemies of parochialism, isolation, fractiousness, war. Market psychology attenuates the psychology of ideological and religious cleavages and assumes a concord among producers and consumers—categories that ill fit narrowly conceived national or religious cultures. Shopping has little tolerance for blue laws, whether dictated by pub-closing British paternalism, Sabbath-observing Jewish Orthodox fundamentalism, or no-Sunday-liquor-sales Massachusetts puritanism. In the context of common markets, international law ceases to be a vision of justice and becomes a workaday framework for getting things done—enforcing contracts, ensuring that governments abide by deals, regulating trade and currency relations, and so forth.

Common markets demand a common language, as well as a common currency, and they produce common behaviors of the kind bred by cosmopolitan city life everywhere. Commercial pilots, computer programmers, international bankers, media specialists, oil riggers, entertainment celebrities, ecology experts, demographers, accountants, professors, athletes—these compose a new breed of men and women for whom religion, culture, and nationality can seem only marginal elements in a working identity. Although sociologists of everyday life will no doubt continue to distinguish a Japanese from an American mode, shopping has a common signature throughout the world. Cynics might even say that some of the recent revolutions in Eastern Europe have had as their true goal not liberty and the right to vote but well-paying jobs and the right to shop (although the vote is proving easier to acquire than consumer goods). The market imperative is, then, plenty powerful; but, notwithstanding some of the claims made for "democratic capitalism," it is not identical with the democratic imperative.

THE RESOURCE IMPERATIVE. Democrats once dreamed of societies whose political autonomy rested firmly on economic independence. The Athenians idealized what they called autarky, and tried for a while to create a way of life simple and austere enough to make the polis genuinely self-sufficient. To be free meant to be independent of any other community or polis. Not even the Athenians were able to achieve autarky, however: human nature, it turns out, is dependency. By the time of Pericles, Athenian politics was inextricably bound up with a flowering empire held together by naval power and commerce—an empire that, even as it appeared to enhance Athenian might, ate away at

Athenian independence and autarky. Master and slave, it turned out, were bound together by mutual insufficiency.

The dream of autarky briefly engrossed nineteenth-century America as well, for the underpopulated, endlessly bountiful land, the cornucopia of natural resources, and the natural barriers of a continent walled in by two great seas led many to believe that America could be a world unto itself. Given this past, it has been harder for Americans than for most to accept the inevitability of interdependence. But the rapid depletion of resources even in a country like ours, where they once seemed inexhaustible, and the maldistribution of arable soil and mineral resources on the planet, leave even the wealthiest societies ever more resource-dependent and many other nations in permanently desperate straits.

Every nation, it turns out, needs something another nation has; some nations have almost nothing they need.

THE INFORMATION-TECHNOLOGY IMPERATIVE. Enlightenment science and the technologies derived from it are inherently universalizing. They entail a quest for descriptive principles of general application, a search for universal solutions to particular problems, and an unswerving embrace of objectivity and impartiality.

Scientific progress embodies and depends on open communication, a common discourse rooted in rationality, collaboration, and an easy and regular flow and exchange of information. Such ideals can be hypocritical covers for power-mongering by elites, and they may be shown to be wanting in many other ways, but they are entailed by the very idea of science and they make science and globalization practical allies.

Business, banking, and commerce all depend on information flow and are facilitated by new communication technologies. The hardware of these technologies tends to be systemic and integrated—computer, television, cable, satellite, laser, fiber-optic, and microchip technologies combining to create a vast interactive communications and information network that can potentially give every person on earth access to every other person, and make every datum, every byte, available to every set of eyes. If the automobile was, as George Ball once said (when he gave his blessing to a Fiat factory in the Soviet Union during the Cold War), "an ideology on four wheels," then electronic telecommunication and information systems are an ideology at 186,000 miles per second—which makes for a very small planet in a very big hurry. Individual cultures speak particular languages; commerce and science increasingly speak English; the whole world speaks logarithms and binary mathematics.

Moreover, the pursuit of science and technology asks for, even compels, open societies. Satellite footprints do not respect national borders; telephone wires penetrate the most closed societies. With photocopying and then fax machines having infiltrated Soviet universities and *samizdat* literary circles in the eighties, and computer modems having multiplied like rabbits in communism's bureaucratic warrens thereafter, *glasnost* could not be far behind. In their social requisites, secrecy and science are enemies.

The new technology's software is perhaps even more globalizing than its hardware. The information arm of international commerce's sprawling body reaches out and touches distinct nations and parochial cultures, and gives them a common face chiseled in Hollywood, on Madison Avenue, and in Silicon Valley. Throughout the 1980s one of the most-watched television programs in South Africa was *The Cosby Show*. The demise of apartheid was already in production. Exhibitors at the 1991 Cannes film festival expressed growing anxiety over the "homogenization" and "Americanization" of the global film industry when, for the third year running, American films dominated the awards ceremonies. America has dominated the world's popular culture for much longer, and much more decisively. In November of 1991 Switzerland's once insular culture boasted best-seller lists featuring *Terminator 2* as the No. 1 movie, *Scarlett* as the No. 1 book, and Prince's *Diamonds and Pearls* as the No. 1 record album. No wonder the Japanese are buying Hollywood film studios even faster than Americans are buying Japanese television sets. This kind of software supremacy may in the long term be far more important than hardware superiority, because culture has become more potent than armaments. What is the power of the Pentagon compared with Disneyland? Can the Sixth Fleet keep up with CNN? McDonald's in Moscow and Coke in China will do more to create a global culture than military colonization ever could. It is less the goods than the brand names that do the work, for they convey lifestyle images that alter perception and challenge behavior. They make up the seductive software of McWorld's common (at times much too common) soul.

Yet in all this high-tech commercial world there is nothing that looks particularly democratic. It lends itself to surveillance as well as liberty, to new forms of manipulation and covert control as well as new kinds of participation, to skewed, unjust market outcomes as well as greater productivity. The consumer society and the open society are not quite synonymous. Capitalism and democracy have a relationship, but it is something less than a marriage. An efficient free market after all requires that consumers be free to vote their dollars on competing goods, not that citizens be free to vote their values and beliefs on competing political candidates and programs. The free market flourished in junta-run Chile, in military-governed Taiwan and Korea, and, earlier, in a variety of autocratic European empires as well as their colonial possessions.

THE ECOLOGICAL IMPERATIVE. The impact of globalization on ecology is a cliché even to world leaders who ignore it. We know well enough that the German forests can be destroyed by Swiss and Italians driving gas-guzzlers fueled by leaded gas. We also know that the planet can be asphyxiated by greenhouse gases because Brazilian farmers want to be part of the twentieth century and are burning down tropical rain forests to clear a little land to plough, and because Indonesians make a living out of converting their lush jungle into toothpicks for fastidious Japanese diners, upsetting the delicate oxygen balance and in effect puncturing our global lungs. Yet this ecological consciousness has meant not only greater awareness but also greater inequality, as modernized nations try to slam the door behind them, saying to developing nations, "The world cannot afford your modernization; ours has wrung it dry!"

Each of the four imperatives just cited is transnational, transideological, and transcultural. Each applies impartially to Catholics, Jews, Muslims, Hindus, and Buddhists; to democrats and totalitarians; to capitalists and socialists. The Enlightenment dream of a universal rational society has to a remarkable degree been realized—but in a form that is commercialized, homogenized, depoliticized, bureaucratized, and, of course, radically incomplete, for the movement toward McWorld is in competition with forces of global breakdown, national dissolution, and centrifugal corruption. These forces, working in the opposite direction, are the essence of what I call Jihad.

Jihad, or the Lebanonization of the World

OPEC, the World Bank, the United Nations, the International Red Cross, the multinational corporation…there are scores of institutions that reflect globalization. But they often appear as ineffective reactors to the world's real actors: national states and, to an ever greater degree, subnational factions in permanent rebellion against uniformity and integration—even the kind represented by universal law and justice. The headlines feature these players regularly: they are cultures, not countries; parts, not wholes; sects, not religions; rebellious factions and dissenting minorities at war not just with globalism but with the traditional nation-state. Kurds, Basques, Puerto Ricans, Ossetians, East Timoreans, Quebecois, the Catholics of Northern Ireland, Abkhasians, Kurile Islander Japanese, the Zulus of Inkatha, Catalonians, Tamils, and, of course, Palestinians—people without countries, inhabiting nations not their own, seeking smaller worlds within borders that will seal them off from modernity.

A powerful irony is at work here. Nationalism was once a force of integration and unification, a movement aimed at bringing together disparate clans, tribes, and cultural fragments under new, assimilationist flags. But as Ortega y Gasset noted more than sixty years ago, having won its victories, nationalism changed its strategy. In the 1920s, and again today, it is more often a reactionary and divisive force, pulverizing the very nations it once helped cement together. The force that creates nations is "inclusive," Ortega wrote in *The Revolt of the Masses*. "In periods of consolidation, nationalism has a positive value, and is a lofty standard. But in Europe everything is more than consolidated, and nationalism is nothing but a mania..."

This mania has left the post-Cold War world smoldering with hot wars; the international scene is little more unified than it was at the end of the Great War, in Ortega's own time. There were more than thirty wars in progress last year, most of them ethnic, racial, tribal, or religious in character, and the list of unsafe regions doesn't seem to be getting any shorter. Some new world order!

The aim of many of these small-scale wars is to redraw boundaries, to implode states and resecure parochial identities: to escape McWorld's dully insistent imperatives. The mood is that of Jihad: war not as an instrument of policy but as an emblem of identity, an expression of community, an end in itself. Even where there is no shooting war, there is fractiousness, secession, and the quest for ever smaller communities. Add to the list of dangerous countries those at risk: In Switzerland and Spain, Jurassian and Basque separatists still argue the virtues of ancient identities, sometimes in the language of bombs. Hyperdisintegration in the former Soviet Union may well continue unabated—not just a Ukraine independent from the Soviet Union but a Bessarabian Ukraine independent from the Ukrainian republic; not just

Russia severed from the defunct union but Tatarstan severed from Russia. Yugoslavia makes even the disunited, ex-Soviet, nonsocialist republics that were once the Soviet Union look integrated, its sectarian fatherlands springing up within factional motherlands like weeds within weeds within weeds. Kurdish independence would threaten the territorial integrity of four Middle Eastern nations. Well before the current cataclysm Soviet Georgia made a claim for autonomy from the Soviet Union, only to be faced with its Ossetians (164,000 in a republic of 5.5 million) demanding their own self-determination within Georgia. The Abkhasian minority in Georgia has followed suit. Even the good will established by Canada's once promising Meech Lake protocols is in danger, with Francophone Quebec again threatening the dissolution of the federation. In South Africa the emergence from apartheid was hardly achieved when friction between Inkatha's Zulus and the African National Congress's tribally identified members threatened to replace Europeans' racism with an indigenous tribal war. After thirty years of attempted integration using the colonial language (English) as a unifier, Nigeria is now playing with the idea of linguistic multiculturalism— which could mean the cultural breakup of the nation into hundreds of tribal fragments. Even Saddam Hussein has benefited from the threat of internal Jihad, having used renewed tribal and religious warfare to turn last season's mortal enemies into reluctant allies of an Iraqi nationhood that he nearly destroyed.

The passing of communism has torn away the thin veneer of internationalism (workers of the world unite!) to reveal ethnic prejudices that are not only ugly and deep-seated but increasingly murderous. Europe's old scourge, anti-Semitism, is back with a vengeance, but it is only one of many antagonisms. It appears all too easy to throw the historical gears into reverse and pass from a Communist dictatorship back into a tribal state.

Among the tribes, religion is also a battlefield. ("Jihad" is a rich word whose generic meaning is "struggle"—usually the struggle of the soul to avert evil. Strictly applied to religious war, it is used only in reference to battles where the faith is under assault, or battles against a government that denies the practice of Islam. My use here is rhetorical, but does follow both journalistic practice and history.) Remember the Thirty Years War? Whatever forms of Enlightenment universalism might once have come to grace such historically related forms of monotheism as Judaism, Christianity, and Islam, in many of their modern incarnations they are parochial rather than cosmopolitan, angry rather than loving, proselytizing rather than ecumenical, zealous rather than rationalist, sectarian rather than deistic, ethnocentric rather than universalizing. As a result, like the new forms of hypernationalism, the new expressions of religious fundamentalism are fractious and pulverizing, never integrating. This is religion as the Crusaders knew it: a battle to the death for souls that if not saved will be forever lost.

The atmospherics of Jihad have resulted in a breakdown of civility in the name of identity, of comity in the name of community. International relations have sometimes taken on the aspect of gang war—cultural turf battles featuring tribal factions that were supposed to be sublimated as integral parts of large national, economic, postcolonial, and constitutional entities.

The Darkening Future of Democracy

These rather melodramatic tableaux vivants do not tell the whole story, however. For all their defects, Jihad and McWorld have their attractions. Yet, to repeat and insist, the attractions are unrelated to democracy. Neither McWorld nor Jihad is remotely democratic in impulse. Neither needs democracy; neither promotes democracy.

McWorld does manage to look pretty seductive in a world obsessed with Jihad. It delivers peace, prosperity, and relative unity—if at the cost of independence, community, and identity (which is generally based on difference). The primary political values required by the global market are order and tranquillity, and freedom—as in the phrases "free trade," "free press," and "free love." Human rights are needed to a degree, but not citizenship or participation—and no more social justice and equality than are necessary to promote efficient economic production and consumption. Multinational corporations sometimes seem to prefer doing business with local oligarchs, inasmuch as they can take confidence from dealing with the boss on all crucial matters. Despots who slaughter their own populations are no problem, so long as they leave markets in place and refrain from making war on their neighbors (Saddam Hussein's fatal mistake). In trading partners, predictability is of more value than justice.

The Eastern European revolutions that seemed to arise out of concern for global democratic values quickly deteriorated into a stampede in the general direction of free markets and their ubiquitous, television-promoted shopping malls. East Germany's Neues Forum, that courageous gathering of intellectuals, students, and workers which overturned the Stalinist regime in Berlin in 1989, lasted only six months in

Germany's mini-version of McWorld. Then it gave way to money and markets and monopolies from the West. By the time of the first all-German elections, it could scarcely manage to secure three percent of the vote. Elsewhere there is growing evidence that glasnost will go and perestroika—defined as privatization and an opening of markets to Western bidders—will stay. So understandably anxious are the new rulers of Eastern Europe and whatever entities are forged from the residues of the Soviet Union to gain access to credit and markets and technology—McWorld's flourishing new currencies—that they have shown themselves willing to trade away democratic prospects in pursuit of them: not just old totalitarian ideologies and command-economy production models but some possible indigenous experiments with a third way between capitalism and socialism, such as economic cooperatives and employee stock-ownership plans, both of which have their ardent supporters in the East.

Jihad delivers a different set of virtues: a vibrant local identity, a sense of community, solidarity among kinsmen, neighbors, and countrymen, narrowly conceived. But it also guarantees parochialism and is grounded in exclusion. Solidarity is secured through war against outsiders. And solidarity often means obedience to a hierarchy in governance, fanaticism in beliefs, and the obliteration of individual selves in the name of the group. Deference to leaders and intolerance toward outsiders (and toward "enemies within") are hallmarks of tribalism—hardly the attitudes required for the cultivation of new democratic women and men capable of governing themselves. Where new democratic experiments have been conducted in retribalizing societies, in both Europe and the Third World, the result has often been anarchy, repression, persecution, and the coming of new, noncommunist forms of very old kinds of despotism. During the past year, Havel's velvet revolution in Czechoslovakia was imperiled by partisans of "Czechland" and of Slovakia as independent entities. India seemed little less rent by Sikh, Hindu, Muslim, and Tamil infighting than it was immediately after the British pulled out, more than forty years ago.

To the extent that either McWorld or Jihad has a *NATURAL* politics, it has turned out to be more of an antipolitics. For McWorld, it is the antipolitics of globalism: bureaucratic, technocratic, and meritocratic, focused (as Marx predicted it would be) on the administration of things—with people, however, among the chief things to be administered. In its politico-economic imperatives McWorld has been guided by laissez-faire market principles that privilege efficiency, productivity, and beneficence at the expense of civic liberty and self-government.

For Jihad, the antipolitics of tribalization has been explicitly anti-democratic: one-party dictatorship, government by military junta, theo-cratic fundamentalism—often associated with a version of the *Fuhrer-prinzip* that empowers an individual to rule on behalf of a people. Even the government of India, struggling for decades to model democracy for a people who will soon number a billion, longs for great leaders; and for every Mahatma Gandhi, Indira Gandhi, or Rajiv Gandhi taken from them by zealous assassins, the Indians appear to seek a replace-ment who will deliver them from the lengthy travail of their freedom.

The Confederal Option

How can democracy be secured and spread in a world whose primary ten-dencies are at best indifferent to it (McWorld) and at worst deeply anti-thetical to it (Jihad)? My guess is that globalization will eventually van-quish retribalization. The ethos of material "civilization" has not yet en-countered an obstacle it has been unable to thrust aside. Ortega may have grasped in the 1920s a clue to our own future in the coming millennium.

"Everyone sees the need of a new principle of life. But as always happens in similar crises—some people attempt to save the situation by an artificial intensification of the very principle which has led to decay. This is the meaning of the 'nationalist' outburst of recent years...things have always gone that way. The last flare, the longest; the last sigh, the deepest. On the very eve of their disappearance there is an intensifica-tion of frontiers—military and economic."

Jihad may be a last deep sigh before the eternal yawn of McWorld. On the other hand, Ortega was not exactly prescient; his prophecy of peace and internationalism came just before blitzkrieg, world war, and the Holocaust tore the old order to bits. Yet democracy is how we re-monstrate with reality, the rebuke our aspirations offer to history. And if retribalization is inhospitable to democracy, there is nonetheless a form of democratic government that can accommodate parochialism and communitarianism, one that can even save them from their defects and make them more tolerant and participatory: decentralized participa-tory democracy. And if McWorld is indifferent to democracy, there is nonetheless a form of democratic government that suits global markets passably well—representative government in its federal or, better still, confederal variation.

With its concern for accountability, the protection of minorities, and the universal rule of law, a confederalized representative system would serve the political needs of McWorld as well as oligarchic bureaucratism or meritocratic elitism is currently doing. As we are already beginning to see, many nations may survive in the long term only as confederations that afford local regions smaller than "nations" extensive jurisdiction. Recommended reading for democrats of the twenty-first century is not the U.S. Constitution or the French Declaration of Rights of Man and Citizen but the Articles of Confederation, that suddenly pertinent document that stitched together the thirteen American colonies into what then seemed a too loose confederation of independent states but now appears a new form of political realism, as veterans of Yeltsin's new Russia and the new Europe created at Maastricht will attest.

By the same token, the participatory and direct form of democracy that engages citizens in civic activity and civic judgment and goes well beyond just voting and accountability—the system I have called "strong democracy"—suits the political needs of decentralized communities as well as theocratic and nationalist party dictatorships have done. Local neighborhoods need not be democratic, but they can be. Real democracy has flourished in diminutive settings: the spirit of liberty, Tocqueville said, is local. Participatory democracy, if not naturally apposite to tribalism, has an undeniable attractiveness under conditions of parochialism.

Democracy in any of these variations will, however, continue to be obstructed by the undemocratic and antidemocratic trends toward uniformitarian globalism and intolerant retribalization which I have portrayed here. For democracy to persist in our brave new McWorld, we will have to commit acts of conscious political will—a possibility, but hardly a probability, under these conditions. Political will requires much more than the quick fix of the transfer of institutions. Like technology transfer, institution transfer rests on foolish assumptions about a uniform world of the kind that once fired the imagination of colonial administrators. Spread English justice to the colonies by exporting wigs. Let an East Indian trading company act as the vanguard to Britain's free parliamentary institutions. Today's well-intentioned quick-fixers in the National Endowment for Democracy and the Kennedy School of Government, in the unions and foundations and universities zealously nurturing contacts in Eastern Europe and the Third World, are hoping to democratize by long distance. Post Bulgaria a parliament by first-class mail. Fed Ex the Bill of Rights to Sri Lanka. Cable Cambodia some common law.

Yet Eastern Europe has already demonstrated that importing free political parties, parliaments, and presses cannot establish a democratic civil society; imposing a free market may even have the opposite effect. Democracy grows from the bottom up and cannot be imposed from the top down. Civil society has to be built from the inside out. The institutional superstructure comes last. Poland may become democratic, but then again it may heed the Pope, and prefer to found its politics on its Catholicism, with uncertain consequences for democracy. Bulgaria may become democratic, but it may prefer tribal war. The former Soviet Union may become a democratic confederation, or it may just grow into an anarchic and weak conglomeration of markets for other nations' goods and services.

Democrats need to seek out indigenous democratic impulses. There is always a desire for self-government, always some expression of participation, accountability, consent, and representation, even in traditional hierarchical societies. These need to be identified, tapped, modified, and incorporated into new democratic practices with an indigenous flavor. The tortoises among the democratizers may ultimately outlive or outpace the hares, for they will have the time and patience to explore conditions along the way, and to adapt their gait to changing circumstances. Tragically, democracy in a hurry often looks something like France in 1794 or China in 1989.

It certainly seems possible that the most attractive democratic ideal in the face of the brutal realities of Jihad and the dull realities of McWorld will be a confederal union of semi-autonomous communities smaller than nation-states, tied together into regional economic associations and markets larger than nation-states—participatory and self-determining in local matters at the bottom, representative and accountable at the top. The nation-state would play a diminished role, and sovereignty would lose some of its political potency. The Green movement adage "Think globally, act locally" would actually come to describe the conduct of politics.

This vision reflects only an ideal, however—one that is not terribly likely to be realized. Freedom, Jean-Jacques Rousseau once wrote, is a food easy to eat but hard to digest. Still, democracy has always played itself out against the odds. And democracy remains both a form of coherence as binding as McWorld and a secular faith potentially as inspiriting as Jihad.

The Counterterrorist Myth

By Reuel Marc Gerecht

The United States has spent billions of dollars on counterterrorism since the U.S. embassy bombings in Tanzania and Kenya, in August of 1998. Tens of millions have been spent on covert operations specifically targeting Usama bin Ladin and his terrorist organization, al-Qa'ida. Senior U.S. officials boldly claim—even after the suicide attack last October on the USS Cole, in the port of Aden—that the Central Intelligence Agency and the Federal Bureau of Investigation are clandestinely "picking apart" bin Ladin's organization "limb by limb." But having worked for the CIA for nearly nine years on Middle Eastern matters (I left the Directorate of Operations because of frustration with the Agency's many problems), I would argue that America's counterterrorism program in the Middle East and its environs is a myth.

Peshawar, the capital of Pakistan's Northwest Frontier, is on the cultural periphery of the Middle East. It is just down the Grand Trunk Road from the legendary Khyber Pass, the gateway to Afghanistan. Peshawar is where bin Ladin cut his teeth in the Islamic jihad, when, in the mid-1980s, he became the financier and logistics man for the Maktab al-Khidamat, The Office of Services, an overt organization trying to recruit and aid Muslim, chiefly Arab, volunteers for the war against the Soviets in Afghanistan. The friendships and associations made in The Office of Services gave birth to the clandestine al-Qa'ida, The Base, whose explicit aim is to wage a *jihad* against the West, especially the United States.

According to Afghan contacts and Pakistani officials, bin Ladin's men regularly move through Peshawar and use it as a hub for phone, fax, and modem communication with the outside world. Members of the embassy-bombing teams in Africa probably planned to flee back to Pakistan. Once there they would likely have made their way into bin Ladin's open arms through al-Qa'ida's numerous friends in Peshawar. Every tribe and region of Afghanistan is represented in this city, which is dominated by the Pathans, the pre-eminent tribe in the Northwest Frontier and southern Afghanistan. Peshawar is also a power base of the Taliban, Afghanistan's fundamentalist rulers. Knowing the city's ins and outs would be indispensable to any U.S. effort to capture or kill bin Ladin and his closest associates. Intelligence collection on al-Qa'ida can't be of much real value unless the agent network covers Peshawar.

During a recent visit, at sunset, when the city's cloistered alleys go black except for an occasional flashing neon sign, I would walk through Afghan neighborhoods. Even in the darkness I had a case officer's worst sensation—eyes following me everywhere. To escape the crowds I would pop into carpet, copper, and jewelry shops and every cybercafé I could find. These were poorly lit one- or two-room walk-ups where young men surfed Western porn. No matter where I went, the feeling never left me. I couldn't see how the CIA as it is today had any chance of running a successful counterterrorist operation against bin Ladin in Peshawar, the Dodge City of Central Asia.

Westerners cannot visit the cinder-block, mud-brick side of the Muslim world—whence bin Ladin's foot soldiers mostly come—without announcing who they are. No case officer stationed in Pakistan can penetrate either the Afghan communities in Peshawar or the Northwest Frontier's numerous religious schools, which feed manpower and ideas to bin Ladin and the Taliban, and seriously expect to gather useful information about radical Islamic terrorism—let alone recruit foreign agents.

Even a Muslim CIA officer with native-language abilities (and the Agency, according to several active-duty case officers, has very few operatives from Middle Eastern backgrounds) could do little more in this environment than a blond, blue-eyed all-American. Case officers cannot long escape the embassies and consulates in which they serve. A U.S. official overseas, photographed and registered with the local intelligence and security services, can't travel much, particularly in a police-rich country like Pakistan, without the "host" services knowing about it. An officer who tries to go native, pretending to be a true-believing radical Muslim searching for brothers in the cause, will make a fool of himself quickly.

In Pakistan, where the government's Inter-Services Intelligence Agency and the ruling army are competent and tough, the CIA can do little if these institutions are against it. And they are against it. Where the Taliban and Usama bin Ladin are concerned, Pakistan and the

United States aren't allies. Relations between the two countries have been poor for years, owing to American opposition to Pakistan's successful nuclear-weapons program and, more recently, Islamabad's backing of Muslim Kashmiri separatists. Bin Ladin's presence in Afghanistan as a "guest" of the Pakistani-backed Taliban has injected even more distrust and suspicion into the relationship.

In other words, American intelligence has not gained and will not gain Pakistan's assistance in its pursuit of bin Ladin. The only effective way to run offensive counterterrorist operations against Islamic radicals in more or less hostile territory is with "non-official-cover" officers— operatives who are in no way openly attached to the U.S. government. Imagine James Bond minus the gadgets, the women, the Walther PPK, and the Aston Martin. But as of late 1999 no program to insert NOCs into an Islamic fundamentalist organization abroad had been implemented, according to one such officer who has served in the Middle East. "NOCs haven't really changed at all since the Cold War," he told me recently. "We're still a group of fake businessmen who live in big houses overseas. We don't go to mosques and pray."

A former senior Near East Division operative says, "The CIA probably doesn't have a single truly qualified Arabic-speaking officer of Middle Eastern background who can play a believable Muslim fundamentalist who would volunteer to spend years of his life with shitty food and no women in the mountains of Afghanistan. For Christ's sake, most case officers live in the suburbs of Virginia. We don't do that kind of thing." A younger case officer boils the problem down even further: "Operations that include diarrhea as a way of life don't happen."

Behind-the-lines counterterrorism operations are just too dangerous for CIA officers to participate in directly. When I was in the Directorate of Operations, the Agency would deploy a small army of officers for a meeting with a *possibly* dangerous foreigner if he couldn't be met in the safety of a U.S. embassy or consulate. Officers still in the clandestine service say that the Agency's risk-averse, bureaucratic nature— which mirrors, of course, the growing physical risk-aversion of American society—has only gotten worse.

A few miles from Peshawar's central bazaar, near the old Cantonment, where redcoats once drilled and where the U.S. consulate can be found, is the American Club, a traditional hangout for international-aid workers, diplomats, journalists, and spooks. Worn-out Western travelers often stop here on the way from Afghanistan to decompress; one can buy a drink, watch videos, order a steak. Security warnings from the American embassy are posted on the club's hallway bulletin board.

The bulletins I saw last December advised U.S. officials and their families to stay away from crowds, mosques, and anyplace else devout Pakistanis and Afghans might gather. The U.S. embassy in Islamabad, a fortress surrounded by roadblocks, Pakistani soldiers, and walls topped with security cameras and razor wire, strongly recommended a low profile—essentially life within the Westernized, high-walled Cantonment area or other spots where diplomats are unlikely to bump into fundamentalists.

Such warnings accurately reflect the mentality inside both the Department of State and the CIA. Individual officers may venture out, but their curiosity isn't encouraged or rewarded. Unless one of bin Ladin's foot soldiers walks through the door of a U.S. consulate or embassy, the odds that a CIA counterterrorist officer will ever see one are extremely poor.

The Directorate of Operations' history of success has done little to prepare the CIA for its confrontation with radical Islamic terrorism. Perhaps the DO's most memorable victory was against militant Palestinian groups in the 1970s and 1980s. The CIA could find common ground with Palestinian militants, who often drink, womanize, and spend time in nice hotels in pleasant, comfortable countries. Still, its "penetrations" of the PLO—delightfully and kindly rendered in David Ignatius's novel *Agents of Innocence* (1987)—were essentially emissaries from Yasir Arafat to the U.S. government.

Difficulties with fundamentalism and mud-brick neighborhoods aside, the CIA has stubbornly refused to develop cadres of operatives specializing in one or two countries. Throughout the Soviet-Afghan war (1979-1989) the DO never developed a team of Afghan experts. The first case officer in Afghanistan to have some proficiency in an Afghan language didn't arrive until 1987, just a year and a half before the war's end. Robert Baer, one of the most talented Middle East case officers of the past twenty years (and the only operative in the 1980s to collect consistently first-rate intelligence on the Lebanese Hizbollah and the Palestinian Islamic Jihad), suggested to headquarters in the early 1990s that the CIA might want to collect intelligence on Afghanistan from the neighboring Central Asian republics of the former Soviet Union.

Headquarters' reply: Too dangerous, and why bother? The Cold War there was over with the Soviet withdrawal in 1989. Afghanistan was too far away, internecine warfare was seen as endemic, and radical Islam was an abstract idea. Afghanistan has since become the brain center and training ground for Islamic terrorism against the United States, yet the CIA's clandestine service still usually keeps officers on the Afghan account no more than two or three years.

Until October of 1999 no CIA official visited Ahmad Shah Mas'ud in Afghanistan. Mas'ud is the ruler of northeastern Afghanistan and the leader of the only force still fighting the Taliban. He was the most accomplished commander of the anti-Soviet *mujahideen* guerrillas; his army now daily confronts Arab military units that are under the banner of bin Ladin, yet no CIA case officer has yet debriefed Mas'ud's soldiers on the front lines or the Pakistani, Afghan, Chinese-Turkoman, and Arab holy warriors they've captured.

The CIA's Counterterrorism Center, which now has hundreds of employees from numerous government agencies, was the creation of Duane "Dewey" Clarridge, an extraordinarily energetic bureaucrat-spook. In less than a year in the mid-1980s Clarridge converted a three-man operation confined to one room with one TV set broadcasting CNN into a staff that rivaled the clandestine service's Near East Division for primacy in counterterrorist operations. Yet the Counterterrorism Center didn't alter the CIA's methods overseas at all. "We didn't really think about the details of operations—how we would penetrate this or that group," a former senior counterterrorist official says. "Victory for us meant that we stopped [Thomas] Twetten [the chief of the clandestine service's Near East Division] from walking all over us." In my years inside the CIA, I never once heard case officers overseas or back at headquarters discuss the ABCs of a recruitment operation against any Middle Eastern target that took a case officer far off the diplomatic and business-conference circuits. Long-term seeding operations simply didn't occur.

George Tenet, who became the director of the CIA in 1997, has repeatedly described America's counterterrorist program as "robust" and in most cases successful at keeping bin Ladin's terrorists "off-balance" and anxious about their own security. The Clinton Administration's senior director for counterterrorism on the National Security Council, Richard Clarke, who has continued as the counterterrorist czar in the Bush Administration, is sure that bin Ladin and his men stay awake at night "around the campfire" in Afghanistan, "worried stiff about who we're going to get next."

If we are going to defeat Usama bin Ladin, we need to openly side with Ahmad Shah Mas'ud, who still has a decent chance of fracturing the tribal coalition behind Taliban power. That, more effectively than any clandestine counterterrorist program in the Middle East, might eventually force al-Qa'ida's leader to flee Afghanistan, where U.S. and allied intelligence and military forces cannot reach him.

Until then, I don't think Usama bin Ladin and his allies will be losing much sleep around the campfire.

Pakistan and the Taliban

By John Echeverri-Gent

Good foreign policy should consider, not only measures to achieve immediate objectives, but also their second-order consequences. Often times, the United States' pursuit of immediate foreign policy goals has produced unintended consequences that have had disastrous repercussions over the longer term. This is especially true in the case of Pakistan and Afghanistan. The United States, through the CIA, funded and trained the mujahideen, including—according to many reports—Osama bin Laden himself, though this has been denied by the CIA. The United States also turned a blind eye to the support and training given to the Taliban by the Pakistani government. And indeed, when the Taliban came to power in 1996, the Clinton administration—perhaps motivated by the lobbying of UNOCAL, an American oil company that was attempting to build a pipeline from Central Asia through the region—gave indications that it was willing to recognize the Taliban government until stories of atrocities against women and violation of other human rights were widely disseminated. The training of the mujahideen has also greatly contributed to religious fundamentalism in Pakistan, and it is this very religious fundamentalism that poses a threat to the stability of the Pakistani government.

In order to understand the dilemma Pakistan's government faces, we have to think a bit about Pakistan's state and society, the role of the Pakistani regime, and the rise of religious fundamentalism. Along with Israel, Pakistan is one of only two states that were founded after World War II that were created with religion as a raison d'etre. The history of each has in fact been driven by tensions between their religious rationale for existence and the commitment of their founders to secularism. In each, the political power of religious fundamentalism has increased over time.

© *Miller Center Report*, Vol. 17, nr. 4 Fall 2001: pp. 26-30. Courtesy of Miller Center of Public Affairs, University of Virginia.

The legitimacy of the Pakistani state has always been precarious. The leadership of the Muslim League, the party of the Pakistan's founders, came from northern India and had limited organization and support in the territory that is now Pakistan. Mohammad Ali Jinnah, though born in Karachi, lived his adult life in Mumbai. Liaquat Ali Khan was the second most important leader and came from Uttar Pradesh. In essence, the leadership of the Muslim League was a foreign import. In contrast to India, where the leadership of the Independence movement and the Congress Party were able to provide stable leadership for decades after independence, in Pakistan the leadership of the Muslim League were unable to provide stable leadership. They were marginalized by the "Pakistanization" of the political system—a process through which large landowners and local religious leaders played an increasingly important role.

Scholars like Benedict Anderson remind us that the creation of modern nation-states involves a process through which the people's identity is transformed from a mosaic of parochial communities to a unified national community. Pakistan remains in the midst of this transition.

Pakistan is a state with remarkable ethnic diversity. No single language is spoken by a majority of Pakistanis, and Urdu, the national language, is the mother tongue of only 8% of the population. True, Punjabis account for more than 50% of the population, but their control over matters has been resisted by various sub-national movements in the provinces of Sindh, Pakistan's second largest province, and Baluchistan. Pakistan has also had trouble integrating the Muhajirs, or refugees from India, who not constitute a very substantial segment of Pakistan's largest cities. The centralizing proclivities of political leaders like Zulfikar Ali Bhutto and Mian Nawaz Sharif as well as the divide and conquer tactics of the Machiavellian Zia ul Haq have exacerbated ethnic tensions, and ethnic conflict has been a hindrance to the consolidation of the Pakistani state.

Pakistan, as a state, also suffers from a lack of government reach. Most Pakistanis live in the countryside. Yet, the literacy rate—being very low at only 38%—shows a tremendous gap between urban literacy and rural literacy. While approximately 50% of the urban population is literate, only 21% of the rural population is literate. Furthermore, while a majority of the Pakistani population lives in the countryside—approximately 67%—85% of all hospital beds are in urban areas. So clearly, there has been this failure of the state government to reach out and provide the services that are important in building a national identity.

Maintaining law and order is fundamental to the legitimacy of the state. Pakistan's government, whether civilian or military, has had only limited success in this area, especially in the last two decades. The fighting in Afghanistan and the consequent influx of some three million refugees have contributed to the challenge of maintaining law and order. Since the 1980s, Pakistan has seen a rise in illegal drug and arms trade. Pakistani society has become more violent, and there is evidence of criminal influence over some actors in the political system.

Religion plays a divisive role as well. Although about 95% of Pakistanis are Muslim, there has been a history of religious conflict since the 1980s, resulting in political violence between the Sunni majority, which constitutes about 75% of Pakistanis, and the Shia minority, which constitutes about 20%.

Ironically, the military dominance of the state has contributed to, rather than mitigated, Pakistan's instability. The military has ruled Pakistan for longer than there has been civilian rule during the post-independence era. Military rulers have always had to look for ways to bolster their legitimacy. During the 1980s, under the leadership of General Zia ul Haq, the military promoted religious fundamentalism as a means of building political support. American foreign assistance, especially during the war against the Soviets in Afghanistan, strengthened the Pakistani military. It also strengthened the military's Interservices Intelligence—an agency that was responsible for channeling American assistance to the mujahideen groups fighting the Soviets—which some analysts contend often acts like a state unto itself.

Religious fundamentalism is perhaps the biggest threat to Pakistani stability today. During the 1980s, the United States spent approximately $4 billion in Pakistan to promote the mujahideen's fight against the Soviets in Afghanistan. The Saudis spent another $1.5 billion. Now, groups such as the Lakshar-e-Taiba and the Harkat ul Mujahideen, who are currently fighting in Kashmir, have also pledged to fight against the United States. They have also pledged to turn Pakistan into what they call a "truly Islamic state." These groups now have control over substantial military equipment.

The Pakistani government has played an even more important role in promoting these fundamentalist groups. In fact, in the 1980s General Mohammad Zia ul Haq promoted religious education in particular madrasahs, local Muslim religious schools. General Zia promoted these as a way to garner support from religious parties for his rule. General Zia allowed funds gathered through the zakat, or the Islamic tithe collected by the state, to be used to fund the development and expansion of these madrasahs. Increasingly the madrasahs have gained access to funding by private sources: either wealthy Pakistani industrialists; sectarian political parties within Pakistan who are identified with one or another religious group, Sunni or Shia; or sources from the Persian Gulf states, from Saudi Arabia and from Iran. The more access the madrasahs have to private funds, the more they become independent of state control. Pakistan officials themselves estimate that from 10–15% of the country's 45,000 madrasahs espouse extremist—what we might call "jihadi"—ideologies.

Support for fundamentalism in Pakistan is rooted in poverty and ignorance that characterizes the Pakistani countryside. According to the most recent World Bank statistics, about 36% of the Pakistani public—and a much higher rate in rural areas—live below the poverty line. At the same time, Pakistan spends about 30% of its national budget and 5% of its gross domestic product on the military. Pakistan also spends another third of its budget on paying off its deficit. So that leaves only one-third to provide various social services, including education alternatives to the madrasahs.

The spread of religious education, in fact, has exacerbated tensions between Pakistan's Sunnis and Shias, which in turn has fueled the growth of religious militance. In fact, there have been violent sectarian clashes between fundamentalists from the Sunni majority and Shia minority. Sunni organizations received substantial funding from Saudi Arabia and Iraq, while the Shia organizations get funds from Iran. In a real sense, Pakistan's sectarian groups are fighting a proxy war for religious rivalries between these countries.

According to Eqbal Ahmad, Pakistani religious militants have formed Jihad International Incorporated. Different religious groups have been known to hire international criminal rings to do their dirty work. For example, the Dubai criminal ring that bombed the Bombay Stock Exchange in 1993 confessed that they had spent a month training in Pakistan before the bombing. That their passports did not show any demarcation of having spent time in Pakistan, suggest complicity by the Pakistani government. Madrasahs have increasingly become international training grounds or Islamic militants. They are filled by students from Chechnya, Uzbekistan, Tajikistan, Afghanistan, Yemen, Mongolia, and countries as far-fetched as Kuwait, Burma, and Indonesia.

After a Sunni fundamentalist gang attempted to assassinate Prime Minister Nawaz Sharif in Pakistan in 1999, the government of Pakistan attempted to rein in the fundamentalists by setting up military courts to try terrorist crimes. But this effort was rendered largely ineffectual because the Supreme Court declared that these courts were unconstitutional. The government has also tried to implement a "deweaponization plan" to reduce the availability of guns. However, as of July 2001, according to the Home Ministry, this plan has collected only 83,000 out of what is estimated to be several hundred thousand illegal weapons in Pakistani society.

In June 2000, the government announced a new policy to rein in the madrasahs. It required them to:

- register with the government,
- expand their curriculum to include instruction in secular scholarship,
- disclose their sources of financial support,
- secure permission from the Pakistani government for admitting foreign students, and
- stop sending their students to paramilitary training camps.

Implementation of these requirements was largely ineffective. By the spring of 2000, more than a year before the acts of September 11, the State Department announced that South Asia had replaced the Middle East as the leading locus of terrorism in the world.

This history accounts for the dilemma confronting Pakistan. On the one hand, the United States and the Western world have a great deal of economic leverage over the country. The Pakistani economy is still very dependent [upon] foreign assistance. Despite reforms implemented under General Musharraf prior to September 11, Pakistan still has a $37 billion foreign debt, and at one point last year, Pakistan's foreign exchange reserves dipped to less than $1 billion, which covered only four weeks of Pakistan's imports.

On the other hand, Musharraf faces a very difficult domestic political scene. Support for the United States will be vehemently opposed by Pakistan's main religious parties. While Benazir Bhutto's Pakistan People's Party has largely supported Musharraf's alignment with the U.S., all other parties have expressed varying degrees of opposition. The most vociferous opponents have been the religious parties and mujahideen based in Pakistan. One mujahideen leader declared, "If the government allows Pakistan to be used for attacks on Afghanistan...all mujahideen organizations would stand shoulder to shoulder with their Afghan brethren."

In light of these formidable political challenges, the extent of General Musharraf's alignment with the United States has been remarkable. First of all, he quickly agreed to allow the United States access to Pakistani airspace. Second, he has provided Pakistani intelligence on Osama bin Laden. Third of all, he has provided some logistical support, such as refueling facilities, for American troops.

The fight against terrorism is as much a political as a military campaign. We will need to win the support of countries like Pakistan, Afghanistan, and states throughout the Middle East where governments and public opinion are ambivalent about the United States foreign policy. Americans themselves are rightfully concerned about many of these countries whose political institutions contradict American values. This ambivalent context makes the second-order consequences of our actions all the more important. We need to avoid expedient actions that might alienate the support of strategic allies, and we need to pursue policies that minimize the long-term prospects that our very allies produce or host international terrorists.

They're Only Sleeping

By Ahmed Rashid

Why militant Islamicists in Central Asia aren't going to go away.

A few miles outside Dushanbe, the capital of Tajikistan, the road heading north into the Garm Valley is enveloped by the majestic Pamir Mountains. It winds across the valley floor through green fields that are punctuated with poverty-stricken villages, empty factories, and blackened chimney stacks. For the first part of the drive, the valley is broad and open, but higher up it narrows and the road clings precariously to the mountainside, with the Surkhob River thundering below. In villages that hang from sheer, rock-faced slopes, Tajiks dressed in colorful robes tend teahouses that have long wooden benches covered with carpets and cushions. Their patrons are weary drivers of donkey and horse caravans and of ancient, exhaust-spewing, Soviet-era trucks that wend slowly down from the Garm district with fruit and vegetables for Dushanbe's markets. Halfway up the valley, where the river broadens into a magnificent vista, a narrow road leads into the Tavildara Valley. The Garm Valley road continues up to the towns of Garm, Tajikabad, Hoit, and Jirgatal before crossing into Kyrgyzstan.

The Tavildara Valley road has been roughly hewn out of rock faces so steep that the mountain peaks aren't visible above it. Even in spring, the temperatures are often below freezing and the high passes blocked by snow and landslides. The Tavildara Valley was one of the strongholds of the Islamicist guerrillas who fought against government troops during the civil war that was waged in Tajikistan from 1992 to 1997. Some of the biggest battles of the war were fought there. This is ideal guerrilla country, where a handful of men can hold off an army.

Originally published 1/14/2002 issue of The New Yorker. Excerpt from *Jihad: The Rise of Militant Islam in Central Asia* (2002), excerpt from chapter eight, as printed in The New Yorker. Reprinted by permission of Yale University Press.

Halfway down the valley on the left is a long, narrow gorge, at the end of which, in the village of Sangvor, is the fortified camp, logistics base, and permanent garrison of the Islamic Movement of Uzbekistan. Half a dozen men could defend the mouth of the gorge, and attempts to bomb the massive jumble of rocks and overhanging cliffs would be futile. I was there last spring, a few months after Juma Namangani, the military leader of the I.M.U., had spent some time in the valley.

"Every day, there were lines of people coming to see him— Kazakhs, Tajiks, Uzbeks, Kyrgyz, Arabs, Chechens, Uighurs, Pakistanis, and Afghans—they all wanted to join him and do jihad in Central Asia," a farmer in the village of Tavildara told me. "Every day, there were hundreds of people he had to feed and house and give money to," another said. Namangani had also met with many "sleepers," who live inconspicuously in the villages of the region, going about their daily business and waiting for his call to arms. They were in Sangvor to plan for the I.M.U.'s summer offensive.

The biggest event during Namangani's stay was his marriage to his second wife, a local Tajik woman with two sons whose husband had been killed during the Tajik civil war. Hundreds of people attended the wedding feast. The bride was one of the most renowned beauties in the Pamir. Their marriage not only cemented relations with local Tajik clans but also fulfilled a Muslim duty established at the time of the Prophet Muhammad: a marriage to the widow of a shaheed, or martyr in jihad, is doubly blessed.

Juma Namangani is a legendary figure. There are few photographs of him, he doesn't give interviews, and the I.M.U. rarely issues statements to the press. Namangani's stature among Muslims in Central Asia is rather like that of Che Guevara after he disappeared into South America for his last revolutionary adventure. People say that the advance guards of the I.M.U. are beautiful female snipers armed with the latest scopes and night-vision goggles, and that the guerrillas' knapsacks are filled with dollar bills that they distribute to the farmers who feed them. I.M.U. guerrillas have been blessed by Muslim holy men to make their bodies impervious to wounds or, conversely, to keep their bodies sweet-smelling after death.

The I.M.U. is believed to have been funded by Saudis, Pakistanis, Turks, Iranians, and Osama bin Laden. Namangani was one of the most important "foreign Taliban" commanders in northern Afghanistan during the recent fighting there. He led a pan-Islamic force of Uzbeks, Tajiks, Pakistanis, Chechens, and Uighurs from Xinjiang province in

China. They fought on the side of the Taliban in Afghanistan, but their long-range goal was to establish an Islamic state throughout Central Asia.

In mid-November, rumors began circulating that Namangani had been killed by American bombs, but there was no proof that this was so, and the details of the rumors were not consistent—some said that he had been wounded and taken to Kabul, where he died in a Taliban hospital, some that he had been killed in one place or another in the north. Toward the end of the month, after the surrender of the Taliban had been negotiated and the city of Kunduz fell, Namangani's headquarters in Kunduz, a walled compound near the central square, was turned into a Northern Alliance barracks. It had been looted by civilians before the soldiers arrived, but there was still plenty of evidence that it had been used for training recruits in an international Islamic jihad. Manuals in several languages described techniques for operating weapons, rigging booby traps, assembling car bombs.

In late December, the President of Tajikistan, Emomali Rakhmonov, and the President of Uzbekistan, Islam Karimov, held a joint press conference. Rakhmonov claimed that he had "accurate and reliable information" that Namangani was dead. President Karimov was less clear on the issue, although one would think that he would be the first to welcome such evidence. Namangani has been sentenced to death in absentia for subversive activities, murder, and bombings in Uzbekistan. One of the bombings, which took place in 1999, shortly after the I.M.U. was formed, was apparently intended to kill Karimov. The brutal suppression of Muslims in Uzbekistan led to the formation of the I.M.U., and human-rights organizations say that Karimov's regime has accelerated the harassment in recent years.

Juma Namangani is the nom de guerre of Jumaboi Ahmadjonovich Khodjiyev. He was born in 1968 in Namangan, an Uzbek city in the Fergana Valley—the heart of Central Asia. The people of Central Asia are predominantly Sunni Muslims of the Hanafi school. Arab invaders brought Islam to the Fergana Valley in the seventh century, and it has been a hub of Islamic culture and politics ever since. To the west lie the ancient Muslim capitals of Bukhara and Samarkand. The two hundred and forty mosques and one hundred and thirteen madrasahs of medieval Bukhara produced scholars who spread their faith throughout Russia, China, South Asia, and the Middle East.

Russia captured much of modern-day Uzbekistan, Turkmenistan, and Tajikistan in the late nineteenth century, although nomadic tribes resisted Russian rule for several decades, and periodic revolts broke out in the Fergana Valley. To assert control, the Russians began resettling the region with ethnic Russians and Cossacks. They developed vast irrigation projects and turned much of the land over to cotton production. New industries manned by Russian workers were also introduced, and the region was linked with Russia through a railway network that for the first time brought the Russian Empire to the borders of Afghanistan, Persia, China, and British India.

After the Russian Revolution, Central Asians, led by Muslim "Basmachis"—bandits, as the Bolsheviks called them—resisted becoming part of the new Soviet Union. The Basmachis were subdued, more or less, by 1924, and Stalin began redrawing the map of the area into five Soviet republics—Kazakhstan, Kyrgyzstan, Tajikistan, Turkmenistan, and Uzbekistan. The new borders were established not along geographic or ethnic lines but in ways that seemed likeliest to suppress dissent, dividing clans, villages, and ethnic groups. The Fergana Valley was split among three republics. The Tajiks were given their own republic, but it did not contain the Tajik cultural and economic centers, Bukhara and Samarkand, which went to Uzbekistan.

Millions of Central Asians died during the forced land-resettlement and collectivization programs and political purges of the late nineteen-twenties and the thirties. Then, for more than sixty years, Central Asia was cut off from contact with the outside world, as the Soviet Union closed its borders with Iran, Turkey, Afghanistan, and, later, China. Central Asians learned nothing about the ideas that shaped the twentieth century, including developments in Islamic thinking and politics that were taking place just across their borders. Mosques were shut down and converted into workshops, Muslim worship and ceremonies were banned, women were forbidden to wear the veil. People could not even read the Koran.

The government of Uzbekistan opened an officially sanctioned madrasah in Bukhara in 1946 and another in Tashkent, the capital city, ten years later. The Soviets introduced a policy that came to be known to its critics as "official Islam." Mullahs were trained in both Islamic and Soviet studies and then appointed to a registered mosque. But "unofficial" Islam sustained the true faith. Unregistered mosques flourished clandestinely, and itinerant mullahs and fakirs carried out religious rites. The Fergana Valley was home to a large number of unofficial madrasahs, and children from all over Central Asia came there to study.

In the late nineteen-eighties, when perestroika began to take hold in the Soviet Union, there was an explosion of interest in Islam in Central Asia. Thousands of mosques were built, Korans and other Islamic literature were brought in from Saudi Arabia and Pakistan and distributed free among the population, and the itinerant mullahs became public prayer leaders on collective farms and in villages. It wasn't really an "explosion," of course, since Islam had never disappeared, not even during the worst repression of the Soviet era. But there were external factors that contributed to the revival of Islam in this period. And these new factors led to a disturbing trend in Central Asia, one that is still dominant—the rise of Islamic militancy.

After the Soviet Union invaded Afghanistan in 1979, thousands of Central Asians were drafted into the Red Army to fight the Afghan mujahideen. Central Asian Muslims were thus reintroduced to the umma, or Islamic world community, through a war against their co-religionists, and many were deeply affected by the dedication of their opponents. Hundreds of Uzbek and Tajik Muslims travelled secretly to Pakistan and Saudi Arabia to study in madrasahs or to train as guerrilla fighters against the Soviets in Afghanistan.

Many Muslims in Pakistan, Afghanistan, and, later, the Fergana Valley were radicalized in madrasahs run by the Deobandis, members of a Sunni Islam revivalist sect that was established in British India in the nineteenth century. During the late nineteen-eighties, leading Deobandi madrasahs in Pakistan began to reserve places specifically for Central Asian radicals, who arrived without passports or visas and received a free education and a living allowance. The most significant ideological contribution of the Deobandis to Sunni Islam was the revival of the concept of jihad. The Deobandis and the Taliban were especially influential among the generation of militants who later formed the Islamic Movement of Uzbekistan.

The other major Sunni Islam sect that found a foothold in Central Asia was Wahhabism. The strict Wahhabi creed has its roots in an eighteenth-century movement to purify Islam led by Muhammad ibn Abd al-Wahhab. In the twentieth century, it became the official ideology of Saudi Arabia, and after the oil boom in the nineteen-seventies it was a feature of Saudi foreign policy. Although Wahhabis had first arrived in Central Asia in 1912, when a native of Medina, Sayyed Sharie Muhammad, set up Wahhabi cells in the Fergana Valley, their doctrine was at odds with the moderate Islamic traditions of Central Asia, and it was not particularly popular. But in the nineteen-eighties, as Saudi funds flowed to Wahhabi leaders among the mujahideen in Afghanistan and, later, in Central Asia—many of whom trained in Saudi madrasahs—Wahhabism began to play an influential role.

In Uzbekistan, the revival of Islamic militancy began in the city of Namangan while the Soviet Union was collapsing. Several young men from Namangan had forged close ties to Saudi foundations, and late in 1991, with Saudi money and some five thousand young followers, the men established a Wahhabi mosque and a madrasah. The mayor had refused to give them land for the mosque, and they had attacked the headquarters of the Communist Party of Uzbekistan and seized it. The men were led by Tohir Abdukhalilovich Yuldashev, a twenty-four-year-old college dropout and local mullah from the Islamic under-ground. He was aided by Jumaboi Ahmadjonovich Khodjiyev, who later became Juma Namangani. Jumaboi had been conscripted into the Soviet Army and had seen action in Afghanistan as a paratrooper in the late nineteen-eighties. According to some of his friends, his experiences there had turned him into a born-again Muslim.

Yuldashev began to insist that strict Islamic practices be observed in Namangan. People were required to pray regularly, and women had to wear the chador. Yuldashev also set up neighborhood watch commit-tees to combat crime. He demanded, with some audacity, that President Karimov impose Sharia—Islamic law—on the country, and he invited Karimov to debate the issue in Namangan. President Karimov arrived on December 9, 1991, to talk to the militants, but the meeting soon be-came a shouting match. Yuldashev made several impossible de-mands—for example, that Karimov declare Uzbekistan an Islamic state.

Yuldashev's followers were initially members of the Islamic Ren-aissance Party, or I.R.P., which was formed in the Soviet Union in 1990 and was intended to have an independent branch in each Central Asian country, although in Uzbekistan it has never been able to register as a legal party. When the I.R.P. was slow to demand an Islamic politi-cal state, the young militants in Namangan set up the Adolat, or Justice, Party, which called for an Islamic revolution. They had no respect for official Islam, no patience with tradition, and no fear of the political regime, which they considered to be on the verge of disintegration and collapse.

Government ministers in Tashkent told me that in the beginning they had no idea who the militants were or what they wanted—they didn't even know what Wahhabism was. Finally, however, the government cracked down on Adolat. Twenty-seven of its members were arrested in March, 1992. Yuldashev fled to Tajikistan and studied for a short time at a madrasah in Dushanbe, but in May civil war broke out in Tajikistan between the government and opposition groups that included Islamicists, democrats, and nationalists. He left for Afghanistan and helped spread I.R.P. propaganda from there, but he soon began to travel, first to Pakistan and Saudi Arabia and later to Iran, the United Arab Emirates, and Turkey, making contact with other Islamic parties. He also met with intelligence agencies in these countries. Pakistan's Inter-Services Intelligence, which had helped run the Afghan war against the Soviets and later supported the Taliban, gave Yuldashev funds and a sanctuary.

From 1995 to 1998, Yuldashev was based mostly in Peshawar, the center not only of Pakistani and Afghan Islamic activism but also of pan-Islamic jihadi groups. Here he met with "Arab-Afghans," Arabs who had gone to Afghanistan to fight the Soviets and stayed to fight for Osama bin Laden. Pakistan's Jamiat Ulema Islam Party, which later backed the Taliban, raised funds for Yuldashev in Peshawar and enlisted his young Uzbek activists in its madrasahs. Russian and Uzbek officials claim that Yuldashev also received funding from the intelligence agencies of Saudi Arabia, Iran, and Turkey and from Islamic charities and organizations in those countries. He travelled to the Caucasus, where he met with Chechen rebel commanders and established himself as the spokesman, grand strategist, and spiritual guide for Islamic revolution in Uzbekistan.

According to a former Tajik political activist with the I.R.P., Juma Namangani also fled Uzbekistan in 1992 and went to Kurgan, in southern Tajikistan, with some thirty Uzbek militants and a few Arabs who were acting as liaisons between Saudi Islamic foundations and Adolat. "Within a few months, Namangani's force had swelled to some two hundred Uzbeks, as more young men fled the crackdown in the Fergana Valley and arrived to join him," the activist said. "Arabs from Afghanistan who were fed up with the sickening civil war there"—the fighting among the mujahideen that led to the rise of the Taliban—"also joined him. As a former Soviet soldier, Namangani knew the tactics of the Soviet Army and special forces, which was extremely useful to the I.R.P. because it was dealing with the Soviet-trained army of Tajikistan. He knew all about bombs and mine warfare and used them effectively in ambushes. He had money from the Saudis and contacts with the Afghans, so he was not alone."

The I.R.P. added Tajik guerrillas to Namangani's group and moved him to the Tavildara Valley, which became his base after 1993 and is still the most important I.M.U. base in Central Asia. Namangani captured and lost the town of Tavildara twice during the Tajik civil war. I.R.P. leaders who knew him at the time say that he commanded loyalty from his troops and was a tough disciplinarian and good speaker who could mobilize people, but that he was also erratic, temperamental, and authoritarian. He often flouted orders from I.R.P. political leaders. None of his former friends and allies credit him with much understanding of Islam. "He is essentially a guerrilla leader, not an Islamic scholar," said Moheyuddin Kabir, who was involved in the I.R.P. negotiations with the Dushanbe government that ended the civil war in June, 1997. "He is a good person but not a deep person or intellectual in any way, and he has been shaped by his own military and political experiences rather than by Islamic ideology, but he hates the Uzbek government—that is what motivates him above all. In a way, he is a leader by default, because no other leader is willing to take such risks to oppose Karimov."

Namangani objected to the ceasefire and the peace settlement in Tajikistan. "When the I.R.P. leaders said stop the jihad, Namangani said no," Moheyuddin Kabir said. "His methods of work and aims were only jihad, and he did not have the political flexibility to understand that sometimes compromise is necessary." Eventually, Namangani was persuaded to come down from the mountains. He dispersed most of his forces but retained a core group of Uzbeks and a few guerrillas at his camp in the Tavildara Valley. He settled in Hoit, a small village near Garm, where he bought a large farm and became the owner of several trucks that carried goods to Dushanbe. Some say that to raise funds to keep his organization going and feed his ever-growing entourage at Hoit, Namangani became heavily involved in the transport of heroin from Afghanistan to Tajikistan and on through Kyrgyzstan to Russia and Europe.

Namangani and Yuldashev met at the farm in Hoit to discuss their future. The Tajik civil war had ended; they had lost their bases in the mountains, their manpower, and some of their weapons caches. Several former I.R.P. military commanders were now ministers or senior officials in the Tajik coalition government in Dushanbe, and the I.R.P. did not want to appear to be breaking the ceasefire by continuing to support a small group of Uzbek dissidents. Back home in Uzbekistan, the situation had worsened. Leading Islamicists had been kidnapped and killed by the security forces. "Namangani was now a businessman and a farmer, but every day there were people coming in from all over Uzbekistan—the Fergana Valley, Tashkent, Samarkand—and telling him about atrocities that Karimov was committing," says a businessman in Garm who used to see Namangani once a week when he lived in Hoit.

In 1992, the Uzbek government had begun to use the term "Wahhabi" for anyone who was perceived to be an adherent of radical Islam or who held anti-government sentiments as part of his Islamic beliefs. Five years later, the government was labelling as Wahhabis even ordinary Muslims who practiced Islam in unofficial mosques or who engaged in private prayer or study. Any Muslim who associated with prayer leaders or taught children how to read the Koran was called a Wahhabi. To many, the term came to mean simply persecuted Muslim faithful. President Karimov launched a particularly harsh crackdown against Muslims after an Uzbek policeman was beheaded in Namangan in December, 1997. That same month, the chairman of a collective farm and his wife were also beheaded and three policemen were killed in a shoot-out. Nobody claimed responsibility for the killings, but the government arrested more than a thousand people in the Fergana Valley. Police questioned any man with a beard. Human Rights Watch reported "a government policy of intolerance" toward Muslim believers: arbitrary detentions and arrests, beatings and threats, fabrication of evidence, and torture.

Uzbek refugees arriving at the farm in Hoit put pressure on Namangani and Yuldashev to respond. They agreed to do something, but first they needed a new sanctuary. Tajikistan was no longer a reliable base for their operations. It made more sense to use Afghanistan. Yuldashev had been introduced to the Taliban in Kabul, and they had every reason to offer him refuge: President Karimov was belligerently anti-Taliban, and Uzbekistan was backing the anti-Taliban opposition in Afghanistan. Yuldashev had also met with Osama bin Laden, who was living with the Taliban leaders in Kandahar.

In 1998, Yuldashev settled in Kabul, where the Taliban gave him a house in the diplomatic quarter of Wazir Akbar Khan. He had another house in Kandahar. That summer, he and Namangani formed the Islamic Movement of Uzbekistan. Several months later, on February 16, 1999, six car bombs exploded in the center of Tashkent, in an apparent attempt to assassinate Karimov. The most powerful bomb, set off by two men who jumped from their car and opened fire on police guards before they escaped, exploded at the entrance to the building that housed the office of the cabinet of ministers—one of the most heavily guarded locations in Uzbekistan. Karimov had left his country residence and was on his way to attend a cabinet meeting when his driver was alerted by police that bombs had gone off. Although no officials were harmed, sixteen people were killed and more than a hundred were injured.

Within a few days, at least two thousand people were brought in for questioning. A common theory among Uzbeks is that the bombing was carried out by Karimov's rivals within the regime, but Karimov blamed the Islamicists, claiming that some of the bombers had fled to Pakistan, others to Turkey, and still others to Kazakhstan. Yuldashev was alleged to have organized the assassination attempt from the United Arab Emirates. Throughout the summer, officials in Uzbekistan complained that the Tajiks were harboring Namangani. Although he was clearly there, "harboring" may not have been the best way of describing the situation; Tajikistan was not in a position to take on the I.M.U. Nevertheless, the Tajik President, Emomali Rakhmonov, did exert pressure on I.R.P. leaders in the coalition government to get rid of Namangani or, at the least, to send him to Afghanistan.

When Namangani took up arms in the early summer of 1999, he pledged to the local population and the Dushanbe government that he would not interfere in Tajikistan's politics or attempt to revive the Islamicist movement in Tajikistan; he asked only that he be given transit rights so that he could cross the Tajik-Kyrgyz border into the Fergana Valley. There were few military checkpoints on the roads then, and he was able to use trucks and taxis to transport supplies up the Garm Valley road to Jirgatal, where the goods were loaded onto donkey and horse caravans and sent on treks of four or five days across the mountains and into the foothills at the southern edge of the Fergana Valley. Uzbekistan has mined its borders with Tajikistan and Kyrgyzstan in an attempt to stop the I.M.U., and local villagers who cross the border illegally are arrested. But the border controls have led to a thriving business in smuggling, and many of the smugglers gave the I.M.U. logistical support.

In August, 1999, fearing that Karimov would force the Tajikistan government to attempt to disband his fighters, Namangani took the initiative. In a small village west of Osh, in Kyrgyzstan, a twenty-one-man I.M.U. unit kidnapped a district officer and three Kyrgyz officials, demanding money, supplies, and a helicopter to fly them to Afghanistan in exchange for the hostages. The panic-stricken Kyrgyz government, which was unprepared for such an incursion, quickly succumbed. The hostages were freed after the guerrillas were given safe passage back to Tajikistan. There were persistent reports that the Kyrgyz had also paid them fifty thousand dollars. President Karimov reacted furiously, accusing Kyrgyzstan of collusion with the I.M.U. He sent Uzbek bombers to attack the Jirgatal and Garm districts. Predictably, the destruction sparked protests from Tajikistan and heightened tensions—exactly the kind of interstate conflict that Namangani wanted.

More I.M.U. groups moved into the area around Batken, the most undeveloped district in Kyrgyzstan. Its rich soil has turned to salt because of over-irrigation during the Soviet period and the closing of canals at the Uzbekistan border. Rusting factories have been abandoned, electricity is available for only four hours a day, and there are no jobs. The milk plant, the oil mill, and a wine-making factory have been shut since 1991, and the government has made no attempt to revive them. Guerrillas entered three villages and captured a major general in the Kyrgyz Interior Ministry and four Japanese geologists who worked for a mining agency. As Kyrgyz troops mobilized and Russian military units were sent to try to find the Japanese hostages, four thousand Kyrgyz herdsmen and their families fled the surrounding mountains, creating an enormous humanitarian crisis.

By late August, the I.M.U. groups held some twenty hostages, whom they gradually freed as they fought running battles with the Kyrgyz Army. But they hung on to the Japanese geologists. Several Japanese secret-service agents and diplomats arrived, opening negotiations with neighboring states in an attempt to find a link to the I.M.U. Uzbek planes attacked I.M.U.-held villages around Batken and Osh, killing four Kyrgyz farmers and destroying dozens of houses. The Kyrgyz Army launched an offensive, seeking to cut the guerrilla groups off from one another and drive them back into Tajikistan. The Japanese hostages were finally released in late October. Although both the Japanese and Kyrgyz leaders insisted that no ransom had been paid, Western diplomats reported that Japan had secretly given between two and six million dollars to Kyrgyz officials, who delivered it to the I.M.U.

With winter fast approaching, when the passes into Tajikistan would once more be closed by snow, the I.M.U. retreated to Tavildara. Tajik government ministers from the I.R.P. were already there; they had come to persuade Namangani to go to Afghanistan. In the first week of November, some three hundred I.M.U. militants, along with their wives and children, were escorted across the Afghan border by Russian soldiers. In Afghanistan, they were received by a jubilant Yuldashev and the Taliban. The I.M.U. guerrillas were housed in Mazar-i-Sharif, and their families were moved into a former U.N. refugee camp. The Taliban allowed the I.M.U. to set up a training camp, open political offices in Kabul, Kandahar, and Mazar, and take in fresh recruits who were trickling down from the Fergana Valley. Yuldashev had struck a deal with the Taliban in which the I.M.U. would be free to carry out its military operations against Uzbekistan. In return, the I.M.U. would fight for the Taliban against the forces of Ahmed Shah Massoud, the Defense Minister of the Northern Alliance. For the first time since the Basmachi revolt, the spectre of a military jihad rose across Central Asia.

That winter, Namangani and Yuldashev travelled frequently to Kandahar, where they met with Osama bin Laden and the Taliban leader Mullah Omar to plan strategy and negotiate for arms, ammunition, and money. According to Russian intelligence officials, bin Laden paid for three MI-8 transport helicopters. Namangani reportedly received more than twenty million dollars from bin Laden in the spring of 2000, and his backers in Saudi Arabia and other countries provided another fifteen million for high-tech equipment like sniper rifles, communications devices, and night-vision goggles. Bin Laden's growing links with the I.M.U offered him a new base of operations in Central Asia—an area where previously he had had few contacts.

Much of the I.M.U.'s financing came from the lucrative opium trade through Afghanistan. Ralf Mutschke, the assistant director of Interpol's Criminal Intelligence Directorate, estimated that sixty per cent of Afghan opium exports were moving through Central Asia and that the "I.M.U. may be responsible for seventy per cent of the total amount of heroin and opium transiting through the area." Wherever the I.M.U. appeared, it was clear that its fighters were never short of funds, and they were careful to pay for all the supplies they took from local villagers. Namangani reportedly paid his guerrillas monthly salaries of between a hundred and five hundred dollars—in U.S. dollar bills. This rumor alone was enough to insure that more recruits would join him from the poverty-stricken Fergana Valley.

In July, 2000, Namangani went back to the Tavildara Valley from Afghanistan with a force of several hundred well-armed men, which he began to move into Uzbekistan and Kyrgyzstan for a new offensive. He spent several months quietly infiltrating fighters into the mountains of the Uzbek province of Surkhandarya, where they built a heavily fortified camp, manned by some hundred and seventy I.M.U. guerrillas. The Uzbek Army had no idea they were there until fighting broke out. Foreign diplomats in Tashkent told me that Uzbek special forces who had been trained by the Russians and had just returned from commando training in the United States were outgunned and outclassed. It took a month of heavy fighting, including aerial bombardment, before the Army was able to storm the camp.

During the operation in Surkhandarya province, Uzbek troops forcibly evacuated more than two thousand people from five villages high up in the mountains. These were ethnic-Tajik herdsmen who for generations had lived far from any town or government control. Their plight became a sorry example of Uzbekistan's ability to alienate and traumatize its own people while trying to deal with the I.M.U. The previous fall, the herdsmen had attempted to alert the Uzbek Army to the presence of armed guerrillas in the mountains, but they were ignored. Once fighting broke out, the Uzbek authorities accused the herdsmen of providing food to the I.M.U. "They're very simple and hospitable people," a resident of the town of Sariasio in Surkhandarya told a reporter. "Anyone who comes their way will be invited in, even if he's got a submachine gun hanging around his neck. What's more, in the mountains there's no work, and if they had the chance to sell something, then, of course, they wouldn't refuse."

The Army destroyed the herdsmen's villages and placed the men in a military camp for two months, where they were given almost nothing to eat. They were relocated to an even more desolate area, where some died of cold and hunger. When, in their naïveté, they asked to see President Karimov to describe their plight to him, they were beaten. One man, Hazratkul Kodirov, gave an interview to the BBC describing the miserable conditions. He was tortured and killed by the Uzbek Army. When the family received his body, his brother reported that his head had been crushed, his arms and legs broken, and at least fifty wounds made on his body by a screwdriver. Seventy-three villagers were eventually charged with subversion, terrorism, and abetting the I.M.U.

In August, ten mountain climbers, four of whom were Americans, were kidnapped by guerrillas in Kyrgyzstan. The guerrillas and their hostages were soon surrounded by Kyrgyz special-forces troops. After several days of pursuit, the Kyrgyz killed six guerrillas, captured two others, and rescued the climbers, whose story later became a magazine article and a book. The fact that Americans were involved in the incident had a lot to do with the decision made shortly thereafter by the U.S. government to declare the I.M.U. a terrorist group.

At the end of October, Namangani withdrew his forces and moved back to Afghanistan. The I.M.U., now based in Mazar-i-Sharif and Kunduz, was fast becoming a pan-Islamic force. It numbered two thousand fighters from Kyrgyzstan, Tajikistan, the Caucasus, and the Chinese Muslim province of Xinjiang. They were becoming experienced in the integrated use of armor, artillery, and airpower, and had been involved in field operations with global jihadi networks like Al Qaeda.

That fall, in Tashkent, Namangani and Yuldashev were sentenced to death in absentia. In December, Namangani crossed into Tajikistan from Afghanistan with a multinational force of about three hundred militants. Karimov again accused the Tajik and Kyrgyz governments of harboring the I.M.U., and cut off their gas supplies in retaliation. He stepped up the mining of Uzbekistan's borders, further disrupting families, villages, and trade. Karimov then started expelling refugees from Tajikistan. These were ethnic Uzbeks who had fled Tajikistan during the civil war. There were thousands of such people.

The government of Tajikistan resented Karimov, particularly since he had given sanctuary to several Tajik dissidents. Nevertheless, under enormous pressure from Uzbekistan and the international community, Tajik ministers went to Tavildara to try and persuade Namangani to return to Afghanistan. He agreed to leave—again under the supervision of Russian border guards. In January, 2001, Russian transport helicopters airlifted Namangani and three hundred men from Tavildara to the Afghan border. Conspiracy theories in the streets, in government ministries, and in foreign embassies in Dushanbe had it that the Russians were playing a double game. While Russia officially opposed the I.M.U., it turned a blind eye to Namangani's forays from Afghanistan because Moscow was trying to pressure Karimov into accepting Russian troops and greater Russian influence in Uzbekistan. The Russians never explained why Namangani was not simply arrested.

As the summer of 2001 approached, governments across the region prepared for another I.M.U. assault, which was not long in coming. In late July, two Army posts on the Tajikistan-Kyrgyzstan border were attacked, and a few days later guerrillas attacked a Kyrgyz television transmitter. The guerrillas had not come from Tajikistan. They were

I.M.U. sleepers in Kyrgyz villages. Namangani appeared to have permanent guerrilla forces in Uzbekistan and Kyrgyzstan and a new, independent command structure that could operate without his presence.

Uzbekistan celebrated the tenth anniversary of its independence from the Soviet Union on September 1st, and as part of an anniversary amnesty President Karimov freed some twenty-five thousand of the sixty-four thousand prisoners in Uzbek jails. The government reduced the jail terms for another twenty-five thousand prisoners, but seven thousand Muslims were not covered by the amnesty.

Pressure from human-rights groups and Western governments had forced Karimov to impose the amnesty, but on September 11th his situation vis-à-vis the international community changed dramatically. Within days of the attacks on the World Trade Center, Karimov was being wooed by Washington, as the United States sought to establish military bases and landing rights in Uzbekistan in preparation for an assault on the Taliban. On September 20th, in an address to Congress, President Bush suggested that the I.M.U. was linked to Osama bin Laden and could be a target for United States counterterrorism efforts.

Central Asian leaders feared that giving the United States overt help in fighting the Taliban would provide a propaganda coup for the I.M.U., allowing it to depict the regimes as lackeys of the Americans. Guerrilla attacks could be justified as retribution for the selling out of national interests and also for allowing an infidel force to be based on Central Asian soil with the sole purpose of conducting a war against Muslims. Shortly after Uzbekistan opened its territory to American forces, the World Bank sent a delegation to Tashkent to discuss new loans. The I.M.U. reacted predictably. In a radio interview on October 9th, Yuldashev said that the I.M.U. was "willing to fight shoulder to shoulder with the Taliban" against their enemies, including Uzbekistan. Karimov's willingness to coöperate with the United States was described as support for the infidels against the believers.

Shortly after the Taliban surrendered in northern Afghanistan, Yuldashev was reported to have been in the fort at Mazar-i-Sharif where hundreds of Taliban prisoners were killed during an uprising. At the press conference in late December, President Karimov said that Yuldashev was most likely now in Pakistan. Namangani may indeed have been killed during the American bombing campaign. Certainly, hundreds of their troops were lost.

Support from Osama bin Laden has ended, and the I.M.U.'s sources of financing from the Uzbek diaspora and Arabs in the Gulf states have been dramatically cut back. But if Namangani and Yuldashev are still alive, they will soon reorganize and begin carrying out acts of terrorism against the Karimov regime and against American targets in the cities of Uzbekistan. In any case, the I.M.U. fighters who have escaped from Afghanistan will regroup, probably among the sleepers who remain in Central Asia, with their secret organizational structure intact. Funds are still available from the heroin trade. The poppy-planting season began in November in Afghanistan, where the new government is unlikely to be stable for years to come, if ever.

Uzbekistan and other Central Asian regimes have made no gesture toward reforming their grotesque record of human-rights abuses. Muslim believers remain in Uzbek jails, elections are a farce, there is not even minimal freedom of the press or of assembly, and torture is commonplace. In this landscape of repression, which appears to many to be sanctioned and rewarded by the United States, the I.M.U. and other radical Islamic parties seeking to end the status quo cannot help but find supporters.

The Globalization of Islam

The Return of Muslims to the West

By Yvonne Yazbeck Haddad

Although there are no reliable statistics on the number of Muslims currently living in the West, a 1986 estimate placed about twenty-three million Muslims in Europe. The majority lived in the Balkans and southeastern Europe; they were Slavic converts and remnants of the Turkish expansion into Albania, Bulgaria, Yugoslavia, and Bosnia or of the westward migration of Tatars into Finland and Poland. More recent Muslim sources speculate that the current estimate of Muslims in western Europe (Austria 100,000; Belgium 250,000; Denmark 60,000; France 3,000,000; Germany 2,500,000; Greece 150,000; Ireland 5,000; Italy 500,000; Luxembourg 1,000; the Netherlands 408,000; Norway 22,000; Portugal 15,000; Spain 450,000; Sweden 100,000; Switzerland 100,000; and the United Kingdom 2,000,000) and the Americas (Canada 250,000; Latin America 2,500,000; and the United States 5,000,000) may be as high as 17.4 million.

The composition of the Muslim communities in various nations of western Europe is in part a by-product of earlier relations established between European nations and the Muslim world as well as the European expansion into Muslim territory during the nineteenth and twentieth centuries. It is also conditioned by the predatory political, economic, and cultural relationships that were developed during the colonial period. Thus the first significant group of Muslims to settle in France in the twentieth century were North African and Senegalese mercenaries who were recruited to fight in French colonial wars, including a group that was the vanguard of the Allied troops that liberated Paris from Nazi occupation. A significant number of harkis, Algerian soldiers who fought with the French colonial government to suppress the Algerian revolution, settled in France after 1962 to avoid reprisals. In Germany early settlers were Tatars and Bosnians, many of whom enlisted in the German army: In the Netherlands the first significant Muslim migration came from its colonies of Indonesia and Surinam, and in Britain they were from South Asia and Africa. The majority of Muslims in western Europe, however, were recruited as temporary guestworkers to relieve the shortage of manual labor during the post-World War II economic reconstruction. The host European countries had the full expectation that imported foreign laborers were a transient commodity, and that once their contracts expired, they would return to their homelands. Since then a large number of asylum seekers and refugees from Albania, Algeria, Bulgaria, Afghanistan, Bosnia, Chechnya, Lebanon, Palestine, Iraq, Iran, and Kashmir have augmented the number of Muslims in the West.

The oil boycott that was declared during the Arab-Israeli war in 1973 precipitated an economic depression and widespread unemployment in Europe. Consequently, European economies underwent a dramatic restructuring that decreased the demand for unskilled labor, as more emphasis was placed on service industries while manufacturing jobs were exported to Asia. These changes exacerbated the unemployment problem in the ranks of the guestworkers. Several European nations, including Germany, France, and the Netherlands, eager to shrink the ranks of the unemployed and to expedite foreign laborers on their way home, offered financial incentives for their repatriation. A few took advantage of the offer, but the majority—faced with the prospects of unemployment in their home country and the lack of future access to the European labor market—decided to stay, preferring the unemployment and welfare benefits of living in Europe. This inadvertently led to a substantial increase in the number of Muslims in Europe, as various governments later allowed family reunification. The policy of thinning foreign labor thus backfired, swelling the ranks of Muslims with unemployed dependents, straining social services as well as the educational systems in the settlement areas. In the process the Muslims were transformed from a collectivity of migrant, predominantly male laborers to immigrant families, from sojourners to settlers, and from transients to citizens. The passage of legislation in the 1970s in most European countries that virtually halted labor migration has led to the creation of Muslim minority communities, who increasingly appear to have become a permanent fixture in western European nations.

The emigration of Muslims during the last quarter of the twentieth century to Europe and the Americas is part of the worldwide movement of people from east to west and from south to north in search of higher education, better economic opportunities, and political and religious freedom. Other emigrants are refugees, often the by-product of Euro-American military or political activities. This movement also includes a smattering of those opposed to the authoritarian regimes that dominate the Muslim landscape. The largest Muslim concentrations in western Europe are in former imperial powers: Britain and France. As an economic powerhouse that attracts many immigrants, Germany also holds a large Muslim population. Each European nation has a particular relationship with its immigrants, which has been influenced by its colonial legacy; its historical memory, and its traditional perception of its former subject people. Each nation is in the process of developing policies and models for the treatment of its newest cit- izens, who put the nation's self-perception of liberal traditions and religious tolerance to the test.

The British model, formalized by the creation of the Commonwealth, permitted citizens of the member nations of the Commonwealth and the colonies to reside in the British Isles. The majority of Muslim immigrants in Britain, for example, came from the Indian subcontinent (Indians, Pakistanis, and Bangladeshis) and Africa. As members of the Commonwealth, they enjoyed the privileges of citizenship and were granted equal political and civil rights, a privilege not available to Muslims in the rest of Europe. Most of the Muslim immigrants are lower class laborers, except for a small number of professionals and a small group of wealthy Arabs from the Gulf oil-producing states who maintain luxury homes in London. More recently, conflicts in various Muslim countries have increased the ethnic mix of the Muslim community in Britain.

Muslims in France are predominantly of Maghribi (North African) origin (from Algeria, Morocco, and Tunisia), who have mostly come after World War II. They also include Muslims from such various Muslim states as Nigeria, Iran, Malaysia, Bosnia, Turkey, Senegal, Mali, and Pakistan. More than 30 percent of Muslims in France are second generation. Because Germany has had extensive diplomatic relations with Muslim nations since Charlemagne, a small number of Muslims have lived in Berlin since 1777. A Muslim cemetery still in use by the Turks was opened at Columbia Dam in 1798 when the Ottoman envoy to Germany; Ali Aziz Effendi, died. When a Muslim society that was organized in Berlin in 1922 with members from forty-one nationalities attempted to construct a mosque, however, it failed because of a shortage of funds. The growth of the Muslim community in Germany; however, is a twentieth-century phenomenon, the result of the guestworkers' decisions not to return to their homelands.

The Muslim population in the Netherlands and Belgium is predominantly made up of Turkish and Moroccan immigrants who were recruited as laborers in the 1960s and 1970s. In the Netherlands it also includes a substantial number of immigrants from Surinam, the former Dutch colony that won its independence in 1975. The pattern for Scandinavian nations is similar except for Finland, which has a tiny minority of Tatar traders and craftspeople who have lived there since the nineteenth century, when it was part of the Russian Empire. Their number has recently increased because of the influx of Somali refugees who arrived by way of Moscow. In Sweden and Denmark, Muslim labor migration came in the late 1960s mainly from Turkey and Yugoslavia. Smaller numbers have come from Morocco, Pakistan, and Egypt. In the 1980s Sweden's liberal policies toward the settlement of refugees augmented the numbers of Muslims by a steady inflow of Iranians, Lebanese, Kurds, and Palestinians. Labor migration to Norway began a decade later than labor migration to other western European countries. The largest number of migrants in Norway are from Pakistan, with small contingents from Turkey; Morocco, Iran, Yugoslavia, Somalia, and India. The majority live around the capital, Oslo.

Muslim emigration to southern Europe came a decade after emigration to western Europe, when the southern economies began to prosper and they changed from labor-exporting to labor-importing nations. The first significant number of Muslims began emigrating to Spain in the 1970s. Muslims had a presence in Sicily as early as the seventh century, however, and dominated the island between the ninth and the eleventh centuries. Vestiges of their history can be seen all the way to northern Italy, where a small Muslim minority continued to live until the nineteenth century. Muslim emigration to Italy is a recent phenomenon that has taken place during the past two decades, spearheaded by students from Jordan, Syria, and Palestine who decided to settle. They were followed by the labor migration from other parts of the Muslim world. More recently, illegal immigrants, mostly Bosnians, Albanians, and Kurds, have been trying to settle in Italy, to the consternation of the other members of the European Union.

In Western nations with a tradition of European immigration—the United States, Canada, Latin America, and Australasia (Australia and New Zealand)—the suitability of Muslims for citizenship was questioned in a variety of ways and eventually somewhat resolved. This has not necessarily lessened the prejudice against their presence. The dominant characteristic of the Muslim population in North America is its diversity, which is apparent in national origin and class as well as in political, Ideological, and theological commitment. The Muslim community in the United States and Canada is composed of several generations of Muslim people who have emigrated in a quest for a better life, beginning in the mid-1870s with groups from Syria, Lebanon, Jordan, and Palestine. A small number of displaced people came from eastern Europe after World War I. The repeal of the Asian Exclusion Act in the 1960s in the United States and the membership of Canada in the British Commonwealth brought a large number of immigrants from Bangladesh, India, and Pakistan. The majority of those immigrants initially admitted were the educated professionals (doctors, Scientists, and engineers) recruited to fill the needs of the technological industry. Immigrants continue today to come from all over the world, including displaced people seeking refuge for political, Ideological, or religious reasons.

Muslim immigrants found freedom in western Europe and North America not only to practice but also to propagate their faith. They have taken advantage of this opportunity and created a variety of missionary outreach activities in various countries. They have also created a corpus of literature geared toward proselytizing. A substantial number of Europeans and Euro-Americans have converted to Islam, including an estimated fifty thousand Germans and one hundred thousand North American "Anglos": Christians, Jews, and agnostics, the majority of whom are women. The largest convert community, however—estimated by various scholars at anywhere between one million to two million—is African American. Their conversion initially came through the teachings of the Nation of Islam, headed by Elijah Muhammad and promulgated by his disciple Malcolm X, who initially promoted a racist theology of black supremacy, a mirror image of the teachings of the Ku Klux Klan. The movement developed in the urban United States as a response to the racism encountered by African Americans who emigrated from the cotton fields of the South to the industrial North. Their relegation to particular working and living spaces in the ghettos consolidated new forms of white supremacy and oppression.

Observers estimate that more than eighty nations in Africa, Asia, and eastern Europe are represented in the mosque community of the United States and that these many groups constitute one ummah (Islamic nation), yet they bring with them a variety of traditions and practices as well as a kaleidoscope of doctrines and beliefs fashioned over time in alien contexts. Members of the community are initially surprised at the discrepancy between the ideals they have appropriated and the reality of their differences. Their similar experience of the West is forging some of them into a community of believers engaged in a process of creating a sense of solidarity through common traditions and seeking common ground in their quest to provide a comfort zone where they can fashion a better future for their children.

Western Immigration Policies

Han Entzinger has identified three European models for the immigration of non-Europeans. The first is the guestworker model, adopted mostly in Germanic countries (Germany, Austria, and Switzerland), in which the presence of the immigrants is considered temporary in perpetuity. The government does not expend any effort to integrate them or their families into the new environment, regardless of the fact that their children are born and raised in these countries and do not appear to have any desire to be repatriated. The second is the assimilationist model that is promoted in France. This model insists that if the immigrants seek to become French citizens, they must eschew their foreign cultural, religious, political, and ideological allegiances and accept and assimilate into the already existing consensus of reality and polity of the prevailing system, shedding all alien characteristics. The French policy of Gallicization expects that the end result of integration is that religious practice is privatized, while each Muslim would become socially and economically assimilated. The third model is the ethnic minority model prevalent in a variety of fashions in the United Kingdom, the Netherlands, Belgium, Luxembourg, and the Scandinavian nations. This model recognizes that the immigrant has an alternative cultural identity that can be preserved and accommodated within the larger context.

In Canada the government has been promoting the idea that it is a multicultural society, providing funds for new immigrants to create ethnic organizations, maintain ethnic cultures, and teach their distinctive languages. The propagation of multiculturalism as a national model was adopted in the hope of circumventing the separatists among the French Quebecois. Questions are currently being asked about whether these efforts have gone too far in creating multiple identities, and whether the ramifications of maintaining ethnicities portend a balkanized Canada, because more than 50 percent of the populations of Toronto, Montreal, and Vancouver are foreign born.

In the United States "Anglo conformity" was perceived as the norm through the nineteenth century. Later scholars defined the United States as a melting pot until it was discovered that there were too many unmeltables. In the 1950s Will Herberg promoted the idea of an America with equal religious conglomerates: Protestant, Catholic, and Jewish. There are currently two paradigms that are competing for adoption; both are controversial, and both have their devoted advocates and detractors. The first is promoted by Christian fundamentalists, some in the Jewish community, and a large number of politicians. It identifies America as grounded in Judeo-Christian values. Its critics note that besides infringing on the idea of separation of religion and state, this model tends to maintain the current power structure, confining Buddhists, Hindus, Muslims, and a host of other faiths and values to the periphery. The second model advocates a pluralistic society that celebrates difference. This has raised the fear of the division of America according to ethnic identities, or "grievance groups," with the potential loss of a cohesive identity shared by all Americans, one that is commensurate with the demands of the only superpower in the world.

The situation of Muslims in western Europe and North America, however, is by no means static. New legislation that constrains and manipulates immigration and citizenship laws has been adopted at a fast pace since the 1970s by Western countries in an effort to stem the tide of immigration. They are driven by a variety of factors. Some countries are governed by economic necessities, given the fact that high labor costs and technological innovation in the West have reshaped European and North American economies. At the same time, most of these countries are experiencing a great deal of pressure on the resources of the welfare state because they have an aging population. They are also influenced by political considerations, given the dramatic rise in racist tendencies in a number of nations.

In Britain the government issued the first measures restricting immigration in 1962, but the restrictions did not apply to those who held British passports, which included citizens of the Commonwealth. As the flow of immigrants did not abate, the government found it necessary to institute additional measures in 1968. As a consequence, those seeking to emigrate had to prove that they had connections to a family in Britain before they were allowed into the country. In 1976 the Race Relations Act recognized ethnic communities and their right to be different, thus providing rights for Muslims by prohibiting indirect discrimination based on race. It did not provide for equal rights based on religious affiliation, however....

Muslims and the Challenge of Life in the West

Muslims have emigrated to Western nation-states that have a fully developed myth of national identity, which has been inculcated in the citizens over two centuries through schools and codified through legends and a particular reading of history. This identity has shaped several generations of Europeans and Americans through the cauldron of two world wars. It has been celebrated in literature, art, music, and dance. The nation-states have fashioned distinctive identities based on collective assumptions, promoting a particular worldview that includes a core of values and attitudes that are taken for granted as unique to a superior West. At the same time, the process of nation building has delineated what is considered alien, strange, and weird.

Immigrants have also been shaped in their home countries by the particular events and perceptions of their generation. Most of the adults among them have a pre-formed distinctive identity not only of their tribe, village, town, or city but also of a national identity instilled by the schools and the institutions of the state from which they emigrated. This identity provides the immigrants with a particular understanding of who they are and what their relationship is to the state in which they live; it therefore conditions their understanding of events and reality. Immigrants also bring a pre-formed understanding of Western culture based on a particular interpretation of the shared heritage between the Muslim world and Europe, one that is particularly focused on the recent experience of colonialism and neocolonialism. These perceptions are enhanced and shaped by Western movies and television, which tend to depict Western society as imbued with drugs, violence, racism, and pornography. Muslims who come from societies that favor strong family solidarity are repelled by what they see as a degenerate Western society consumed by premarital and extramarital sex, burdened by a high rate of divorce and births to unmarried women, latchkey kids, and fragile family bonds. They condemn Western values as lacking in the responsibilities of parents and children toward one another, and they believe that Western society puts too much emphasis on individual freedom and not enough on corporate responsibility.

The formation of Muslim minority communities in the West by choice became problematic to some Muslim intellectuals, especially those from India, where "minorityness" involves the survival of Islam under non-Muslim rule. The late Mawlana Abul Ala Mawdudi, who traveled all over Europe, the United States, and Canada, admonished Muslims to avoid integration into their new environment or to leave lest they lose their souls in the West's wayward ways. Other scholars have insisted that such opinions are misguided because the proper interpretation of Islamic law allows Muslims to live outside the abode of Islam, as long as they have the freedom to practice and propagate their faith. Still other scholars are of the opinion that Muslim presence in the West provides them with an unprecedented opportunity to fulfill their Islamic duty to propagate the faith. In the process they not only obey God's commandment to call people to Islam, they also help to redeem Western society from its evil ways and to restore it to the worship of God. The empowerment of Muslims overseas and the propagation of the Islamist ideology as normative for the world should supersede personal gain.

For Zain el-Abedin, the founder of the Institute for Muslim Minority Affairs in Jidda, Saudi Arabia, the greatest challenge the Muslims face in the West is the loss of identity in an alien social and ideological context. The fear is that in its eagerness to fit in, the minority community reluctantly but steadily gives up its cherished values, while the hostile environment slowly but surely chips away at its core beliefs. To protect the community from disintegration, Abedin determined that it was necessary to promote Islam as an ethnicity and in the process erect ramparts not only to keep the aliens out but, more important, to hold the Muslims in. He was aware that this was not an easy task given the diversity of the community. He thus identified important ideological constructs as well as behavioral distinctions as indispensable markers of the cultural divide. He therefore called for the creation by consensus of a particular body of ideals, values, aspirations, goals, and doctrines. While crucial in setting the Muslim community against other worldviews, the ideals in themselves are not sufficient, nor is such a task easy, because Muslims must "squarely confront the reality of the modern secular, multinational state." While maintaining the unquestioned primacy of allegiance to Islam, Muslims in the West thus need to determine the proper attitude toward the new social reality in which they live. Also to be determined is the nature and extent of their commitment to and participation in the new environment. In the process they must clearly identify the ideological constraints that impede full participation in the economic and social spheres, fully cognizant of the consequences of adhering to a precise and ideologically exclusive stance. They also need to "see how some of the political and social effects of this stance can be softened and mitigated and learn to live with those that cannot." There must be an individual as well as a corporate willingness to pay the price for the decision to live on the social, political, and economic margins of society.

Abedin promoted the idea of fashioning Islam as an ethnicity defined by religion, admittedly a rather difficult task because most immigrants have been fashioned by the nation-state from which they came and identify with its causes and feel particular allegiances to ethnic and linguistic preferences and racial origins. The West thus becomes a laboratory in which a new modern identity is to be fused, one that fosters particular behavioral patterns and promotes a common language, distinctive customs and traditions, and recognizable styles of dress and food, among other cultural distinctions. These are easier to identify and particularize than the effort to inculcate ideas because they are more tangible. At the same time, Abedin was aware that ethnicity could be very divisive, given the diversity of migrant groups. The difficulty is in determining whose language, customs, or behavior is more Islamically legitimate. Abedin was aware of the dilemma his recommendations posed for Muslims because on a very important level, ethnicity itself is un-Islamic. Although cultural distinction promotes cohesion and functions as a barrier to being absorbed or assimilated into a multicultural society, it may also veer from the truth of Islam, which affirms that "physical traits, cultural traditions, dress, food, customs, and habits are subordinate or subsidiary to their main doctrinal identity, that God created differences in people in order to facilitate recognition, that the true identity is determined by the manner in which a person or group of any race, colour or physical type approaches the business of living, uses his faculties, selects ends and means for his worldly endeavours."

Khalid Ishaque of Britain is under no illusion that the host societies are about to accept an ideological minority that seeks to maintain its self-respect by promoting commitments and priorities that are deliberately incompatible with those of the host culture. Thus the community must realize that suffering is not only inevitable, but it is to be welcomed in some cases because it provides the opportunity to demonstrate the commitment to a higher cause and walk in the footsteps of the early Muslim community, who were persecuted for their faith, under the leadership of the Prophet Muhammad in Mecca. Ishaque notes that Muslims who choose to live in nations that are not governed by Islamic law should realize that they must assume certain obligations. While accepting adversity, they must constantly endeavor to establish a relationship with the majority that will foster an atmosphere conducive to the propagation of Islam, in which the larger society is receptive to the Muslim solutions to the problems of humanity.

By the 1990s there began to be a shift in the perspective of leaders of the Islamist movement on this issue. Azzam al-Tamimi of Britain, for example, recently identified the reality facing Muslims living in the West as a state of crisis. He feels that the options fostered for Muslims in the West in the 1970s have not succeeded. His assessment is that although not all of the obstacles in the relations of Muslims and non-Muslims in Western societies are brought about by Muslims, the more dangerous and difficult ones are the consequences of Muslim perceptions and behavior. Some Muslims erroneously seek to overcome these obstacles by melting into Western culture and abandoning some or all of their Islamic identity. Others insist on avoiding these obstacles by resorting to isolation and hiding in cocoons, which some fear could eventually form ghettos similar to those occupied by the Jewish communities in previous centuries. For al-Tamimi this discrepancy in dealing with the crisis led to the sundering of relations between the generations. On the one hand is the generation of the fathers, mothers, and grandparents, who have an emotional and cultural tie to the original homeland, who hold on to the same customs and traditions whether or not they accord with the new environment. On the other hand is the generation of the children and grandchildren, who have no emotional ties to the homeland and find little of value in those customs, which are seen as counterproductive, an impediment to progress in the society in which they have been born.

The new Muslim presence in Europe has made some Europeans more self-consciously reflective about being European. Ignoring the history of immigration into Europe over the centuries, the tendency of scholars and politicians is to depict European nations as unique, cohesive, and integrated societies with distinguishing pre-formed and established characteristics. The presence of Muslims who are able to exercise their political rights in Britain as citizens and the possibility of granting citizenship to these Muslim immigrants and their children in Germany; France, and other European countries has become a contentious matter. At the same time, the recent encounter has also made

Muslim immigrants more reflective about their identity, as a growing number have become more self-consciously Muslim. Many who would not have entered a mosque in their homelands have become active in the mosque movement in the West and are increasingly defining the mosque as the center around which Muslim life should revolve. They seem to seek refuge in religion, rummaging through tradition for identifying proper belief, and eager to Islamize behavior, demeanor, and lifestyle as well as to erect cultural boundaries.

For a growing number of Muslims, strict adherence to ritual practice in the adopted country marks the boundaries of distinction. Announcing the need for a clean space for daily prayer, the act of praying, refraining from eating pork and improperly slaughtered meat, and fasting during the month of Ramadan have become important self-delineated boundaries that help the Muslim immigrant feel secure, distinct, and outside the bounds of pollution. For some, conforming to Islamic prohibitions has become a conscious act of witness of a distinctive faith despite public ridicule and a demonstration of steadfastness and perseverance in the face of social obstacles. For others the act of affirming uniqueness itself has become an important affirmation of the need to uphold their identity despite the pressure to change and to abandon the faith. It is a declaration that not only is difference normal, but in a most important way it is divinely designed, approved, and sanctioned. Some Muslims will not associate with other Muslims who do not practice these rituals. Those Muslims are deemed as being outside the pale. Inculcating this message in Muslim children is a mechanism to keep them within the fold. Thus for some, the ritual is Islam and Islam is the ritual....

Muslims and Politics in the West

Regardless of their growing numbers in Europe and North America, and their increasing wealth in the United States and Canada, Muslims are aware that they have little political power to influence the government, the media, or the elites in the West. They have very few channels of communication to policy makers in the societies in which they live. A variety of factors hamper effective participation in the political process, including the lack of experience in participating in political activities, the fear of the consequences of political involvement, and the lack of experience in grassroots organizations or coalition building. Muslims also lack seasoned leaders and efficient organizations that are able to forge coalitions with other groups to bring about change and to influence legislation. This is generally ascribed to a lack of experience in Western-style democracy, which is based on compromise, which many Muslims believe to be tantamount to abandoning the principles of justice and truth. There are external factors as well; among them is their belief that Muslims in the West are often shunned by political candidates and parties as a perceived liability, because their participation might antagonize the Jewish lobby. Democratic presidential candidates have turned down Arab-American endorsements for fear of alienating Jewish support.

The issue of participation in the political process is now being debated within the Muslim community. Can a Muslim participate in the running of a *kuffar* (unbelievers) society? Should they vote for representatives who are accountable to various interests? Would such participation lead to defending the freedom to engage in things Islamically prohibited? Ali Kettani, a North African consultant to the Saudi government on Muslim minority affairs, has called for Islamic political representation: "Otherwise, Muslim politicians would be put in office by non-Muslim forces and would consequently be used to subjugate the Muslim community." The political interests of the immigrant generation are generally focused on the countries left behind. The second generation demonstrates more interest and savvy in local politics. Younger Muslims in Britain, for example, are increasingly involved in British politics. Their interests focus on antiracist and antideportation organizations. They have also worked on campaigns for legislation to allow family reunions and to fight police violence.

In Birmingham, Muslim political participation is mostly aimed at the local level. In 1982 the first Muslim labor representative to the ward was elected. The following year the number increased by two, and by 1987 the first Muslim woman was elected. Many Muslims in Britain vote for the Labour Party because many are laborers and would therefore benefit from the party's programs. In 1984 a Muslim charter appeared recommending that Muslims vote for those who would support their agenda concerning schools, sex education, Muslim personal laws, and provisions for Muslims in state schools. Nothing came of it; nor has the call for the establishment of a Muslim parliament. In Britain local authorities run social services, housing, leisure, and community services, public health programs, and economic, urban development, and equal opportunity programs. Most Muslim concerns are tackled on the local level. In 1993 there were twelve Muslim councilors of 117 in Britain, all members of the Labour Party.

In the Netherlands consultative ethnic minority councils were established in various areas, especially in the major cities where immigrants congregate: Amsterdam, Rotterdam, the Hague, and Utrecht. The councils are recognized by the authorities as representing the community, thus they have to be consulted on matters of interest to minorities. Under the minorities policy, immigrants were extended new rights in the 1980s that included such matters as providing for proper Islamic burial rites and halal slaughtering of animals, to the consternation of animal rights advocates. They were allowed to be employed in the civil service, except for positions in the police and the armed forces. Although they maintain their foreign citizenship, immigrants were granted the right to vote in local elections but could not participate in provincial or national elections. During the local elections of 1986 and 1990, a few foreigners were elected to municipal councils.

In the United States initial political activity came as a result of the Arab-Israeli conflict. American government support for the state of Israel, conjoined with a press that is generally considered by Muslims as acting as a gatekeeper suppressing any reports that would show Israeli policies in a negative light while promoting what is considered a defamation of Arabs, led to the development of Arab political action groups. Their activities have generally centered around three areas: providing accurate information to the American public about Arab culture, history, and religion; challenging and correcting the prevalent negative stereotypes of Arabs and Arab Americans; engaging with U.S. policy makers who seek a more equitable and balanced American policy in the Arab world, especially in regard to the Arab-Israeli conflict. The American-Arab University Graduates was founded in 1967 by professionals, university professors, lawyers, and doctors, a large number of whom had participated in the Organization of Arab Students, which flourished on U.S. campuses in the late 1950s and early 1960s. The targeting of Americans of Arab background by the Nixon administration gave the impetus to the formation of the National Association of Arab Americans, organized in 1972 and modeled after the pro-Israeli lobby, the American Israel Public Affairs Committee. Its aim was to create access to members of the U.S. Congress and to explain the issues from an Arab perspective, while educating Arab Americans about the political process.

The American-Arab Anti-Discrimination Committee, modeled after the Anti-Defamation League of the B'nai B'rith, was established in 1980 to fight racism, prejudice, and discrimination against Arabs in the United States. Founded by James Aburezk, a former U.S. senator from South Dakota, it continues to be the largest grassroots Arab organization in the United States, with chapters in various parts of the country. Its efforts focus on issues of interest to the community, from seeking to halt the production and distribution of movies that vilify Arabs and Muslims by Walt Disney Productions to helping immigrants unjustly targeted for deportation by the U.S. Immigration and Naturalization Service. It has sought apologies from television anchor Dan Rather and former secretary of state Henry Kissinger for defamation and ethnic slurs, filed legal suits to stop certain advertisements that traded on racist sentiments, and more recently advocated the lifting of the U.S. ban on travel to Lebanon and of the siege of Iraq.

The Arab American Institute (AAI) was established in 1984 by James Zoghby; who was active in Jesse Jackson's presidential campaign in 1988. Zoghby was appointed as national co-chair of the campaign and was able to raise $700,000 for Jackson's campaign. The AAI encourages participation in the political system and is eager to get Arab Americans to run for office. The institute establishes Democratic and Republican clubs in various parts of the country.

All Arab American organizations include both Christians and Muslims. In the 1980s several Muslim political action committees were formed, including the American Muslim Council, the Council for American-Islamic Affairs, and United Muslims of America. Their work generally parallels that of the Arab American organizations. They restrict their activities to Muslim rather than Arab concerns and cast a wider net of interest, including the fate of Muslims in Cyprus (Kibris), Kashmir, Bosnia, Kosovo, Bulgaria, and Somalia, among other locales. These political action committees have been recognized as representative institutions of the Muslim community. The leadership has been invited to the White House for Islamic celebrations; they have also co-sponsored petitions and issued statements with non-Muslim political and religious organizations.

The Muslim Presence: Positing a Challenge for the West

The Muslim presence in western Europe and the Americas has posited a challenge and raised concerns that need to be addressed by both the immigrants and the host nations. These issues touch on such social and cultural matters as shifting demographics, race, class, religion, and ethnicity and challenge the very premise of democracy itself, because they impinge on areas of power sharing, law, education, and public policy. Muslim immigrants in the West are noted for their diversity. Their experiences of the West vary according to what beliefs, perceptions, and conditioning they acquired before their emigration as well as the environment into which they settled. Their experiences and their responses are conditioned by the reasons they chose to emigrate, their educational background, and their social class, as well as the historical relationship between their country of origin and the nation into which they have moved. This relationship is also influenced by the policies of the host country: whether it welcomes foreigners and grants them citizenship rights, its perceptions of Islam, and its national policies governing the relationship between religion and state.

Muslim identity in the West is influenced by the dynamic interaction between the variety of conscious and unconscious perspectives that the immigrant brings and the context in which he or she settles. It is also the by-product of the compromises with the host culture that become necessary to lead a coherent life. The immigrant's perspective is dependent on the background from which he or she comes, the class, the experience of social mobility, the level of education, whether he or she is a settler, a refugee, or a sojourner. It is also fashioned by the political identity and the religious perspective on which the immigrant was raised. These factors are constantly renegotiated and refashioned in a society that is perceived and experienced as racist and anti-Muslim, with certain sectors in it engaged or exclusively dedicated to demonize or fan distortion and fear. It also makes a difference whether the individual sees himself or herself as a born-Muslim, a born-again Muslim, or a convert; or whether he or she is defined by ethnic origin, nationality, place and language of origin, and by religious affiliation (Sunni, Shii, Ahmadi, Wahhabi, Alawi, Druze).

Although some Muslims continue to contemplate the option of returning to their homelands as a safety valve should conditions become intolerable, their children, born and reared in the schools of the

West, are caught in the middle: The West is their homeland. They are bicultural, with an intimate experience and knowledge of the West, as well as an intimate experience of their parents' culture as remembered and reinvented in the West. For the immigrants the struggle to maintain their identity and to preserve it from disappearing into the Western culture appears to be an ongoing project. They are increasingly challenged and changed, as their children are becoming more indigenized into Western culture. This has brought about new interpretations by a few daring people who attempt to be relevant to the new reality in which they find themselves. The question is whether they can develop a rational means of minority jurisprudence to guide their lives in the West. If it is developed, the next question is whether the Muslims in the majority nations will recognize such jurisprudence as authentic and valid.

Meanwhile, some Western authors have continued to question whether Muslims are worthy of citizenship in a democratic nation or whether their presence will put their particular stamp on Europe and America, forever changing the West as it is known. Some European scholars fear that Muslims' presence in a multicultural environment will erode Europe's unique identity and make it similar to what exists in the United States or Canada. Still others deny that Muslims are a variable that will make a difference in reshaping Europe. They do not see any difference in the impact of their presence than what has happened in earlier migrations of poorer populations, such as the Poles and Italians. It is clear from the shrill tone of some of those engaged in the debate about whether Muslims belong *in* the West that they are fully aware that Muslims have become part and parcel *of* the West.

Still to be addressed is the Muslim demand for accountability for Western imperialism, as well as the demand that the West come to terms with Islam and recognize its equal status with Christianity and Judaism as a legitimate monotheistic religion. Will the pluralism and democratic principles espoused by both Europe and North America make room for a different culture and allow its members to operate with respect and dignity? Once again, the Muslim presence challenges Europeans not only to reflect on their self-assured perceptions of their liberalism, pluralism, democracy, and tolerance; it has also challenged Europeans to think of ways that they can guarantee the Muslims freedom of religion and the right to propagate their faith and enjoy the culture of their choice. Muslims continue to ask whether Western democracies are liberal enough to include Islamic input into the national consensus, or will there be an insistence on a Judeo-Christian culture. Will

Western pluralism or multiculturalism be flexible enough to provide for Islamic input into the shaping of the future of Western society? Or will Muslims continue to be marginalized, ostracized, studied, and evaluated, always judged as lacking, always the "other"?

Finally, will the juggernaut of assimilation that has reshaped Europe and North America in a long process of secularization, modernization, and liberalization be able to reshape Muslims to the extent that they can dissolve into the Western mix, abandoning their distinctive identities, practices, and cultures? Or will they opt for integration, holding on to their distinctive identities and preferences, at the same time participating in the political and social life of their adopted countries, demanding equal rights, and proportional representation as a distinct group? The questions are not only concerned with what would happen to the Muslims when they choose between assimilation, integration, or separation, but, more important, the questions are also concerned with the manner in which Muslims' integration, assimilation, or separation would affect the Fabric of Western society. What kind of a society will Europe and America become as a consequence of the introduction of the new mix of peoples and cultures who affirm a vibrant religion that they insist transcends borders and supersedes all other claims to truth?

Suggestions for Further Reading

Books:

- Fouad Ajami, *The Arab Predicament: Arab Political Thought and Practice Since 1967* (1992).
- Benjamin Barber, *Jihad vs. McWorld: How Globalism and Tribalism are Reshaping the World* (1995).
- Peter L. Bergen, *Holy War, Inc.: Inside the Secret World of Osama bin Laden* (2001).
- Yossef Bodansky, *Bin Laden: The Man Who Declared War on America* (1999).
- Geraldine Brooks, *Nine Parts of Desire: The Hidden World of Islamic Women* (1995).
- John K. Cooley, *Unholy Wars: Afghanistan, America and International Terrorism.* (2000)
- John L. Esposito, ed., *The Oxford History of Islam* (1999).
- Thomas L. Friedman, *The Lexus and the Olive Tree: Understanding Globalism* (2000).
- Larry P. Goodson, *Afghanistan's Endless War: State Failure, Regional Politics and the Rise of the Taliban* (2001).
- James F. Hoge Jr. and Gideon Rose, eds., *How Did This Happen? Terrorism and the New War* (2001).
- R. Stephen Humphreys, *Between Memory and Desire: The Middle East in a Troubled Age* (1999).
- Samuel Huntington, *The Clash of Civilizations and the Remaking of World Order* (1998).

- Mark Juergensmeyer, *Terror in the Mind of God: The Global Rise of Religious Violence* (2000).
- Elaine Landau, *Osama Bin Laden: A War Against the West* (2002).
- Walter Laqueur, *The New Terrorism: Fanaticism and the Arms of Mass Destruction* (1999).
- Bernard Lewis, *Islam and the West* (1993).
- Bernard Lewis, *What Went Wrong: Western Impact and Middle Eastern Response* (2001).
- Judith Miller, *God Has Ninety-Nine Names: Reporting from a Militant Middle East* (1996).
- Paul R. Pillar and Michael H. Armacost, *Terrorism and U.S. Foreign Policy* (2001).
- Ahmed Rashid, *Jihad: The Rise of Militant Islam in Central Asia* (2002).
- Ahmed Rashid, *Taliban: Militant Islam, Oil and Fundamentalism* (2001).
- Simon Reeve, *The New Jackals: Ramzi Yousef, Osama bin Laden, and the Future of Terrorism* (1999).
- Edward Said, *Covering Islam: How the Media and the Experts Determine How We See the Rest of the World* (1997).
- Strobe Talbott and Nayan Chanda, eds., *The Age of Terror: America and the World after September 11th* (2002).
- Robin Wright, *Sacred Rage: The Wrath of Militant Islam* (2001).

Online Resources:

- www.theatlantic.com
- www.foreignaffairs.org
- www.economist.com
- www.guardian.co.uk
- www.latimes.com
- www.newsweek.com
- www.nytimes.com
- www.salon.com
- www.slate.com
- www.time.com
- www.washingtonpost.com
- www.newyorker.com

The Editor

Fredrik Logevall is Associate Professor of History and co-director of the Cold War History Group at the University of California at Santa Barbara. His publications include: *Choosing War: The Lost Chance for Peace and the Escalation of War in Vietnam* and the *Encyclopedia of American Foreign Policy* (co-editor). A recipient of the the UCSB Academic Senate Distinguished Teaching Award, Logevall lives in Santa Barbara with his wife and two children.